INVESTING WISELY

Register This New Book

Benefits of Registering*

- ✓ FREE **replacements** of lost or damaged books
- ✓ FREE **audiobook** – *Pilgrim's Progress,* audiobook edition
- ✓ FREE information about new titles and other **freebies**

www.anekopress.com/new-book-registration
*See our website for requirements and limitations.

INVESTING WISELY

How to Better Steward Your Wealth

DAVID N. JOHNSON
& J. A. JOHNSON

www.jwealth.co

www.genesisbibleinstitute.org

Investing Wisely

© 2025 by David N. Johnson & J. A. Johnson

All rights reserved. Published 2025.

Securities and Advisory Services offered through Prospera Financial Services. Member FINRA/SIPC.

Cover Designer: J. Martin

Cover Image: iStock/Pineapple Studio

Editor: C. Miskimen

Aneko Press

www.anekopress.com

Aneko Press, Life Sentence Publishing, and our logos are trademarks of

Life Sentence Publishing, Inc.
203 E. Birch Street
P.O. Box 652
Abbotsford, WI 54405

BUSINESS & ECONOMICS / Personal Finance / Investing

Paperback ISBN: 979-8-88936-513-6

eBook ISBN: 979-8-88936-514-3

10   9   8   7   6   5   4   3   2   1

Available where books are sold

To my wife, Lisa, who has been my steadfast partner and greatest supporter for the past forty-five years. Her unwavering encouragement has fueled my passion for helping others live with purpose and leave a legacy – by educating and equipping them to wisely manage their time, treasures, and talents.

Together, we have been blessed to raise three wonderful daughters and, at the same time, build a successful wealth management firm, but this book's deepest dedication belongs to my nine young grandchildren, who stand at the very beginning of their futures. My hope and prayer is that the insights within these pages serve as a guiding light, equipping them with the wisdom they need as they embark on their own life journey to live and leave a legacy.

– Dave Johnson

For my beautiful grandchildren Brooklynn, Harlym, Deuce, Bronx, Ellis, and Shiloh. You make my heart happy.
– J. A. Johnson

Contents

Foreword

When I was a Major League umpire, I got used to being yelled at and jeered, even when I made the right call. In those moments, I would calmly say to myself, "Father, forgive them; they know not what they boo." Over the years, I became fond of getting booed because it verified that I was doing the right thing. As strange as it may sound, those boos were often my assurance that I was calling balls and strikes exactly the way they were supposed to be called – by the book.

In much the same way, investing wisely means doing what is right even when it is not popular. It is sticking to principles when others are chasing shortcuts or momentary wins.

There are plenty of books about building wealth that swing and miss, but *Investing Wisely: How to Better Steward Your Wealth* knocks it out of the park. This book is not just about making money – it is about understanding your role as a steward of everything God has entrusted to you: your income, your investments, your time, your talents, and your influence.

In my career behind the plate, I was the chief steward of the game, responsible for upholding the rules and preserving the integrity of baseball. That was no small task, especially during the five World Series I was blessed to umpire as the crew chief. The stakes were high, and my mission was clear: call the game fairly and faithfully, without favoritism and without compromise.

That is the same charge we each have as stewards of God's resources. The apostle Paul reminded us: *It is required of stewards that they be found faithful* (1 Corinthians 4:2). Faithfulness means doing what is right even when no one is watching – or when everyone is booing.

In *Investing Wisely,* you will find more than practical financial advice. You will discover timeless biblical principles that help you see money not as an end but as a tool – a tool you can use to bless your family, advance God's kingdom, and serve your neighbors. This book calls us to steward everything we have – because, ultimately, none of it belongs to us. It all belongs to God.

As you read these pages, remember that life is not a game, but we are required to play by the rules God has set. Let this book be your playbook for wise, faithful decisions that enable to you to build lasting wealth, honor the Lord, and reflect the faithfulness of the ultimate Crew Chief of heaven and earth. May you find the courage and conviction to make the right calls, even when the crowd does not understand.

Play ball – and invest wisely.

– Dr. Ted Barrett
Former Major League Umpire
Crew Chief, Five World Series
Faithful Steward of the Game – and of God's Calling

Preface

Stewarding God's Resources for Kingdom Impact

We live in a world where money often reigns supreme – where wealth is measured in bank balances, portfolios, and possessions. But as followers of Christ, we are called to a different standard. Fundamentally, money is not ours. Everything we have – every dollar, every possession, every opportunity – is a gift from God. Scripture reminds us: *The earth is the LORD's and the fullness thereof, the world and those who dwell therein* (Psalm 24:1). King David said plainly: *Both riches and honor come from you, and you rule over all. All things come from you, and of your own have we given you* (1 Chronicles 29:12, 14).

Many years ago, I had an experience that etched this truth into my heart. It was a Sunday morning in 1990. Lisa and I sat in church, holding hands and trying to keep our three little ones settled as a missionary couple stepped forward to share about their work overseas.

We were a young married couple, just trying to make ends meet. I had recently started an entry-level job in banking – enough to pay the bills but not enough to get ahead. Like many young families, we lived paycheck to paycheck, with only a modest emergency fund in our account.

As the missionary couple spoke, something began to stir in me. Their stories of lives being transformed and the gospel reaching those who had never heard it moved my heart. But more than that, I sensed God speaking directly to me – not audibly but unmistakably. He said, "Give everything." Specifically, everything in our checking account.

I leaned over and whispered to Lisa what I believed the Lord was prompting. She looked at me and, without hesitation, said, "Then you better not argue with God."

To be clear, our account did not hold a fortune, but it was what we depended on to bridge the gap until the next payday. Still, when the offering plate passed by, I placed a check inside for the full balance. It was not reckless. It was obedience. We walked out of church that day with a strange sense of peace, knowing we had participated in something far bigger than ourselves.

The next day, I went to work as usual. That afternoon, Lisa called. "There is a letter from the IRS in the mailbox," she said. My heart sank. *What if I had miscalculated last year's return? Was this a notice of an error or, worse, a demand for repayment?* I told her not to open it – I would take care of it when I got home.

That evening, I opened the envelope with cautious dread, but what we found inside brought us to our knees.

The letter explained that the IRS had reviewed my tax return and discovered an error – in our favor. They had recalculated the return and were issuing us a refund.

When we saw the check, we gasped.

It was *exactly ten times*, to the penny, what we had given the day before.

We laughed. We cried. We worshiped. God did not just provide – He overwhelmed us with His faithfulness. That moment became a milestone in our journey with Him. It was as if the Lord was saying, "You can never outgive Me."

But that was not the end of the story.

Just a few months later, I was offered a position as a financial advisor. That simple act of obedience in giving became the doorway into a thirty-five-year career where I have had the privilege of helping others steward their resources wisely and generously for God's kingdom.

Even more remarkably, later that year, that same missionary organization invited me to join their board of trustees. I also became their financial advisor, helping them steward the very resources that were growing through the generosity of others – resources that have since funded orphanages, hospitals, seminaries, and churches across multiple countries.

That Sunday morning offering, small by worldly standards, became a seed. God took it, multiplied it, and used it to transform not only our finances but the entire trajectory of our lives and ministry. And through it all, one truth has anchored our journey: *Everything we have belongs to God.* Every dollar, every opportunity, every ounce of wisdom or success – it all comes from Him. We are not owners; we are stewards.

That is the heartbeat of *Investing Wisely*. We wrote this book to help believers view money not as a treasure to hoard but as a tool to steward. Whether you are a young adult, new to investing, or simply seeking a biblical framework for managing God's resources, this book will guide you through seven critical decisions that will transform the way you think about saving, spending, investing, and giving. You will learn timeless principles to help you break free from the pull of consumerism and equip you to live as a faithful steward in a world that often encourages the opposite.

The seven decisions we present in the book are simple, but they are not easy. They require discipline, prayer, and a heart fully surrendered to God's purposes. As you make them, you will learn to make money your servant rather than your master. You will begin to see the value of saving diligently and investing strategically – not for personal gain but to bless others and support the work of God's kingdom.

This book is more than just teaching – it is training. Inside, you will find practical tools to help you put these principles into action:

- **Exhibit 1** is a crash course in the stock market – a quick and clear introduction for anyone new to investing.

- **Resource 1** is a budget worksheet to help you track your income and expenses and commit to a saving and investing plan.

- **Resource 2** is a goal-setting workshop designed to clarify your short-term, mid-term, and long-term financial and stewardship goals.

In addition, you will find a **Study Guide** at the end of the book – perfect for small groups or personal reflection – to help you dig deeper into the principles and apply them to your daily life.

I pray that this book inspires you not only to manage your money wisely but also to embrace an eternal perspective – where your time, treasures, and talents are invested in blessing others and building God's kingdom. May you discover that faithful stewardship is not a burden but a pathway to lasting joy, meaningful purpose, and eternal reward.

– Dave Johnson, Founder
Johnson Wealth Management
www.jwealth.co

Acknowledgments

No book is ever written alone. We are deeply grateful to several friends from our Genesis College family and team who made meaningful contributions to this book.

Special thanks to B. K. Woolsey and J. D. Valvano for their thoughtful feedback and contributions, which strengthened the book in ways we could not have done on our own.

Dawn Little – so often the unseen presence behind many Genesis College courses and projects – helped us bring this book together.

Jess Soprano, as she does with many Genesis projects, made timely updates and improvements.

And finally, Judy "The Closer" Fry ensured that the last draft was complete, polished, and ready to go.

Thank you all. This book is better because of you.

Introduction

I've always believed in the power of story – especially stories of real people who rise above adversity, turn their lives around, and live with purpose. That's exactly what this book delivers. *Investing Wisely* is not just a financial manual – it's a compelling invitation to live differently, think differently, and steward your life and resources for something far greater than yourself.

I've known Dave Johnson for many years, both as a ministry partner and as the Mellon family's trusted financial advisor; and I can tell you this: he doesn't just teach these principles – he lives them. With decades of experience guiding individuals and families through financial uncertainty and into stability and legacy-building, Dave has poured the very best of his wisdom into these pages. What you hold in your hands is the result of a lifetime of faithfulness – not only in financial markets, but in marriage, family, ministry, and calling.

In my own journey as a business owner for 50 years – having operated many McDonald's franchises across Arizona and California – I learned the value of systems, discipline, and long-term vision. But I also learned that wealth without wisdom can quickly become a burden rather than a blessing. That's why this book matters so much. It bridges biblical truth with real-world financial strategy in a way that's practical, faithful, and transformational.

The stories throughout this book are powerful. From Michael, a man in prison who chose to save and invest in the middle of incarceration, to everyday families making sacrificial decisions to give, serve, and build for the future – these are not theoretical examples. They are living proof that wise stewardship is possible for everyone, regardless of background, mistakes, or current income. God honors those who honor Him, and this book shows what that looks like in real time.

Investing Wisely challenges us to stop seeing money as our master and instead use it as a tool to glorify God, bless others, and leave a meaningful legacy. It reminds us that stewardship isn't just about wealth – it's about worship. It's about choosing to live with eternity in mind, making decisions today that will matter forever.

Whether you're a young adult trying to build a solid financial foundation, a couple planning for retirement, a leader guiding others in biblical principles, or someone seeking a second chance at life – this book has something for you. It's a trustworthy guide, rooted in Scripture and tested by experience.

I'm honored to commend this work to you. May it inspire you to take the next faithful step toward becoming the steward God created you to be – generous, wise, bold, and eternally focused.

– Don Mellon
Former Owner of 21 McDonald's Franchises in AZ and CA

Michael's Story

This book is not just about money. It is about change – lasting, legacy-building, God-honoring change. And change does not require wealth or a perfect background. It requires faith, discipline, and a willingness to start where you are. That is why we begin with the story of Michael – a man who started with nothing but an eight-year prison sentence and a turning point.

His story is not just inspiring – it is a roadmap. It is proof that these principles of stewardship and wise investing we are about to introduce apply to anyone willing to make tough decisions and stick to them, even in the most unlikely places.

A Typical Money Waster

Prior to his arrest and conviction, Michael lived paycheck to paycheck. He made enough to own a nice car and rent an apartment, but he spent every cent on himself and his girlfriend. Like many people today, he did not have a savings account or any financial investments.

So, when he made poor choices that sent him to prison, he entered with nothing.

Even after his girlfriend broke up with him and stopped sending money, Michael continued to spend recklessly. His mom, however, faithfully put money in his account, which he quickly drained on snacks, music, and movies. Michael spent more than $150 per month in an attempt to comfort himself and make his prison sentence feel bearable.

The Power of a Verse

Near the end of that first year, Michael was sitting on his bunk watching TV. As he flipped through the channels, he paused on a preacher's sermon, and a Bible verse filled the television screen: *House and wealth are inherited from fathers* (Proverbs 19:14).

Michael could not get those words out of his head. The verse struck him deeply. He had a son he loved dearly and already felt the weight of guilt for being an absent father. But now it hit him even harder – he wasn't leaving "house and wealth" or anything of value to his son.

That verse was a turning point. It set in motion decisions that would shape the rest of Michael's life. Many of those decisions mirror the principles we discuss in this book. He learned to save, sacrifice, invest, and build wealth – starting from nothing.

Making Changes

The first thing Michael did was change his view of money. He realized that his old view of money as something to be spent had held him back. He saw money as a tool to get whatever he wanted in the moment, not as a resource to steward for the future. But that attitude was robbing him of the opportunity to be the kind of father he wanted to be. His encounter with Proverbs 19:14 made him realize he needed to stop squandering money and instead use it purposefully to create a legacy for his son.

Michael adamantly saved money. Prisoners do not control many areas of their lives, but they do control their actions and attitudes. Michael decided to make a financial commitment – something entirely within his power. He developed a one-track mind when it came to his savings plan. He cut out his frivolous spending, determined to live off the food provided in the chow hall.

Michael set a clear financial goal: to save $2,000 per year. This was a challenge, but he knew it would be achievable if he were disciplined. His mom continued to make small contributions every few months. Michael did the math and realized that if he could consistently save $2,000 each year (and with moderate investment growth), he could leave prison with $20,000 or more – a life-changing foundation for his family's future.

To reach that goal, he worked in the kitchen for 35 cents an hour and tapped into his creativity to make extra money. He began making jewelry boxes out of cardboard and newspaper dowels, painting them to look like wood grain. He also learned to craft intricate dollhouses. He sent these handicrafts to his mom, who sold them online through Etsy and eBay for as much as $80 apiece. Both he and his mom were amazed as the sales picked up and the money began to roll in.

As Michael's inmate trust account grew through his prison job and crafts, he faithfully filled out money disbursement forms each month to send the money home. His mom saved every penny he sent, combining it with the money from the craft sales.

After reaching his first $1,000 in savings, Michael had his mom invest the money in a brokerage account with the Vanguard Group. He had learned about online investment platforms from a financial podcast and discovered he could start investing in the stock market with no minimum deposit.

Michael did not walk out of prison a millionaire, but he did leave with an investment portfolio already working for his future – something he had never imagined.

A Father's Legacy

Putting his son's future first transformed how Michael viewed money and responsibility. He developed habits of saving, sacrificing, and investing, determined to one day leave his son a true inheritance. While other inmates spent their days watching television or playing video games, Michael spent his time working in the kitchen and making craft items to sell. While others blew their money on movies and snacks, Michael saved and invested.

Michael developed habits that put him in a position to leave an inheritance to his children – and more importantly, to show his son what it means to be a man who provides, plans, and sacrifices for the good of others. He learned that true wealth is not just about money – it is about passing on values that will outlive you.

Many of us will not waste our money in a prison commissary, but we do on Target runs, in Amazon carts, and on luxury upgrades. You can squander $1,500 as fast as $150. Without knowing how to delay gratification, stay out of debt, invest your savings, and pass on a legacy to your children, the results will be the same whether you are in prison or in a penthouse.

Michael did not wait for better circumstances. He started where he was, with what he had because stewardship is not just about money. It is about redeeming your time and your money to build a legacy that will bless generations to come. Your journey can begin with your next decision.

Chapter 1

Money Is a Tool, Not a Treasure

For where your treasure is, there your heart will be also.
– Jesus (Matthew 6:21)

This book is for individuals who are serious about preparing for their future – people who recognize that if they continue to live as they do now, they will always live paycheck to paycheck and never have sustainable wealth.

You most likely picked up this book because you want to save money, build wealth, and begin preparing for retirement. The seven decisions we explore in this book will equip you to do just that. As you will discover, wealth building is not just for a select few – anyone can do it – but if you want to do so in a way that honors God, you must make several decisions. These are not casual, halfhearted decisions; they require resolve and intentionality. But if you make them, they will radically transform your life and equip you to take the steps needed to build the financial means that will enable you to bless others.

The first decision begins with how we view money and wealth. There is a subtle but dangerous shift that can happen in our hearts when money moves from being a means to an end – and quietly becomes the end itself. It starts with good intentions – saving for a house, planning for the future, or working hard for a promotion. But over time, money can begin to shape our decisions, define our goals, and even determine our sense of worth. The more we accumulate, the more we can begin to feel secure, significant, or even superior. If left unchecked, money becomes more than a resource – it becomes a rival for our worship.

Jesus spoke frequently about the dangers of wealth, not because money is inherently evil, but because He knew our hearts are prone to misplacing our trust. That is why He said, *"For where your treasure is, there your heart will be also"* (Matthew 6:21). When we forget that God is the provider and sustainer, we begin to cling to money with closed fists instead of holding it with open hands. But when we see money as a servant – not a master – we can use it with wisdom to meet needs, bless others, and give to the work of the Lord.

At the heart of biblical stewardship is the call to invest in what matters most – God's kingdom. While every chapter in this book points to this ultimate goal, we give special attention to this principle in Chapter 6. We encourage you to stay vigilant and, from the very beginning, prioritize giving financially to the Lord's work. Now, let us begin our journey of God-glorifying wealth building.

To become a wise and godly investor, here is the first and foundational decision you must make:

DECISION 1: I will make money a tool, not a treasure.

Money Is an Opportunity to Glorify God

Money is a tool, and like any tool, it can be used for good or bad, depending on how it is handled. Some think of money as inherently evil, but there is no biblical support for this. Money is not the problem. The apostle Paul told us what is: *The love of money is a root of all kinds of evils* (1 Timothy 6:10). Paul condemned the *desire to be rich* (1 Timothy 6:9), which can lead to misplaced priorities, materialism, and a distorted purpose for living.

Even Christians can fall into this trap, so blinded by greed and materialism that they break away from their faith: *It is through this craving [the desire to be rich] that some have wandered away from the faith and pierced themselves with many pangs* (1 Timothy 6:10).

It is important to note that the Bible does not condemn being rich. Scripture includes many examples of faithful people whom God blessed with great wealth. King David was rich. So was Solomon, Abraham, and even Job. God provided those riches, so their money alone cannot be an evil thing. Even today, there are many godly, wealthy men and women, but unlike most other wealthy people, they do not idolize money. Riches are not the affections of their hearts.

One of the biggest problems with the love of money is that it never brings contentment. People who love and crave money are never satisfied. They always want more. King Solomon, the richest man in his day, and possibly ever, said, *He who loves money will not be satisfied with money, nor he who loves wealth with his income* (Ecclesiastes 5:10). Solomon called the love of money "vanity." It was worthless; it did not last.

Obsession with wealth is dangerous, and so is building confidence in riches. *A rich man's wealth is his strong city, and like a high wall in his imagination* (Proverbs 18:11). King Uzziah amassed land, tribute, and armies and provided security across his kingdom, *for he was marvelously helped, till he was strong. But when he was strong, he grew proud, to his destruction* (2 Chronicles 26:15-16). Hezekiah was another very wealthy king. He had treasure houses for his riches and storehouses filled with grain. But his pride overcame him, and he showed off all his wealth to the Babylonian envoys. In doing so, he incurred God's wrath and the promise that all his stored riches would later be carried away to Babylon (2 Kings 20:12-18).

The danger of trusting in money rather than God is a recurring theme throughout Scripture. Money itself is neutral. It is a tool designed to trade goods and services, a medium of exchange that we need in this world to be good stewards of the earth and glorify God by using it wisely.

In his book, *Business for the Glory of God*, Wayne

Grudem highlights several ways that our use of money can reflect God's character and bring Him honor. He says we glorify God through:

- Investing and expanding our stewardship, imitating God's sovereignty and wisdom

- Meeting our own needs, imitating God's independence

- Giving generously to others, imitating God's mercy and love

- Supporting the church and evangelism, helping to bring others into the kingdom of God.[1]

When pursued with the right heart, building wealth and making wise investments become more than financial strategies. They become spiritual acts of worship.

Wealth Building Should Honor God

Maybe you have never thought about money as a spiritual matter, but Paul reminded us, *Whatever you do, work heartily, as for the Lord and not for men. You are serving the Lord Christ* (Colossians 3:23-24). Whether earning income, investing wisely, or giving generously, every financial decision can honor God if it is done for His glory. Yet, even as we use money for good, we must guard our hearts.

Jesus said, *"No one can serve two masters, for either*

---

1   Wayne Grudem, *Business for the Glory of God: The Bible's Teaching on the Moral Goodness of Business* (Wheaton, IL: Crossway, 2003), 49.

he will hate the one and love the other, or he will be devoted to the one and despise the other. You cannot serve God and money" (Matthew 6:24).

Money is a wonderful servant but a wicked master. If it becomes the object of our trust or desire, it will pull our hearts away from God. That is why we must carefully examine our motives. Scripture reminds us: *The heart is deceitful above all things, and desperately sick; who can understand it?* (Jeremiah 17:9). The true nature of our hearts and desires is unknowable.

It is easy to make self-centered decisions about money and wealth and then justify them by using spiritual language to claim we did it "for God's glory." But we must be honest with ourselves and with God in how we seek and spend riches.

Consumed by Wealth

The Rich Young Ruler had to learn this lesson the hard way. For him, money was not a tool – it was a treasure. We meet him in Mark 10:17-22, where he approached Jesus with an earnest question: *"Good Teacher, what must I do to inherit eternal life?"* Outwardly, he seemed to be the epitome of success. He was wealthy, moral, and spiritually conscious, at least in his own self-assessment. Yet Jesus's response revealed a deficiency that all his possessions and achievements could not cover. Jesus, after listing the commandments that the man had professed to keep, looked at him and loved him, saying, *"You lack one thing: go, sell all that you have and give to the poor, and you will have treasure in heaven; and come, follow me." Disheartened by the saying, he went away sorrowful, for he had great possessions* (Mark 10:21-22).

The problem was not the man's wealth but his heart's attachment to it. The man had boasted of his obedience to the commandments, but he had failed to keep the first one: *You shall have no other gods before me* (Exodus 20:3). Wealth had become his treasure, his god – and it was the one thing he could not surrender to follow Christ. Jesus saw this and exposed it. He did not say that one must be poor to follow Him, but He did make it clear that those who follow Him must not hold anything else in higher esteem.

Jesus's words challenge us: What holds our allegiance and hearts? Is it money, pleasures, or possessions? Or is it Christ?

Making Christ Your Treasure

Even good and necessary pursuits, like wealth building, must never displace or detract from our relationship with Christ. Money is a tool to build true kingdom wealth, and you must steward the resources God has given to you. Paul, writing to Timothy, instructed the wealthy *to do good, to be rich in good works, to be generous and ready to share, thus storing up treasure for themselves as a good foundation for the future* (1 Timothy 6:18-19). God specifically tells the wealthy they are responsible for doing good deeds for others and building up the church. Expenditures that aggrandize this present life without considering eternity are poisonous, so be sure to use wealth *to take hold of that which is truly life* (1 Timothy 6:19).

When Christ is your treasure, your perspective regarding wealth reflects it. Your thoughts, attitudes, and behaviors demonstrate that wealth building is important but only because it holds promise to be used for good and godly purposes.

When Christ is your treasure, you:

1. Live generously.

Generosity reflects the heart of God, who gave His only Son for us (John 3:16). The gospel makes us generous. It loosens our attachment to the things of this world and prompts us to give our time, talents, and treasures to advance God's work throughout the world. These investments carry eternal value.

Serving with your time and skills, whether in the church or in meaningful causes, is as impactful as financial giving. Many community organizations depend on volunteers to carry out their work. Living generously means that we serve others and demonstrate the love of Christ. Through such giving, we align our priorities with kingdom priorities.

2. Trust completely.

Even as we get our finances in order and engage in wealth creation, we recognize and trust that God is our provider. Trust frees us from the anxiety and fear that often accompany financial matters.

If you find yourself constantly worried about your finances or become obsessed with accumulating wealth, it may be time for a heart check. Is Christ truly your treasure? Put your trust in God to lead and guide you, and trust His provision. The writer of Proverbs reminded us: *Trust in the LORD with all your heart, and do not lean on your own understanding. In all your ways acknowledge him, and he will make straight your paths* (Proverbs 3:5-6).

3. Live with eternity in mind.

When Christ is our treasure, our stewardship takes on eternal significance. We see our resources not as ends in themselves but as means to bless others and advance God's kingdom. Our wealth becomes a visible expression of God's love.

Jesus said, *"Do not lay up for yourselves treasures on earth, where moth and rust destroy and where thieves break in and steal, but lay up for yourselves treasures in heaven, where neither moth or rust destroys and where thieves do not break in and steal"* (Matthew 6:19-20). The choices we make in this life either build temporary rewards here or store up eternal treasure in heaven. Believers are a heavenly people. Living with a heavenly perspective minimizes materialistic desires so we can better live here with an eternal focus. *Seek the things that are above, where Christ is* (Colossians 3:1).

Before you move on to the following chapters where you will learn how to create sustainable wealth, we urge you first to decide: *I will make money a tool, not a treasure.* If you do not first commit to using money as a tool for godly stewardship, the remaining decisions you will be challenged to make run the risk of being self-serving rather than God-glorifying.

Money is a tool entrusted to us by God to be used for His purposes. When wealth becomes the driving force of our lives, it stops serving us and instead begins to master us. The result? Wealth becomes the most important thing in our lives and moves us dangerously closer toward our natural tendency to declare ourselves self-sufficient and independent of God. When Christ is no longer our treasure, wealth takes His place and becomes our idol.

Chapter 2

Every Dollar Counts

Go to the ant, O sluggard; consider her ways, and be wise. Without having any chief, officer, or ruler, she prepares her bread in summer and gathers her food in harvest.
– Solomon (Proverbs 6:6-8)

In the first chapter, we learned the importance of having the right attitude regarding money and wealth. Money is to be a tool we use to bring glory to God, not a treasure to esteem and idolize.

Now we will turn to something that should be easy to do in theory, but for many, rarely done: saving money.

For many, as their income increases, so does their spending. People tend to live up to their means, leaving little or nothing left at the end of each month. When the unexpected happens – unforeseen medical bills, car repairs, home repairs, a job loss – our financial stability is shaken, especially if we covered these costs with credit. In those moments, we find ourselves wishing we had prepared during the good times.

But saving is not just about being ready for emergencies. Saving also involves putting your money to work as you build wealth and prepare for your future. Throughout Scripture, God commends foresight and preparation. The Bible even calls us to look to the ant for wisdom, who *prepares her bread in summer and gathers her food in harvest* (Proverbs 6:8). If we choose to prepare for the future today, we will not only have financial resources available later but we will also be able to use those resources to freely serve God and bless others. It is vital to be a good steward of every dollar God blesses us with, disciplining ourselves to spend less than we make and to save or invest the rest.

The second decision you must make to build wealth may be very difficult, but if you make it – and commit to following through – you will be on your way to becoming an effective steward of the money God has entrusted to you.

DECISION 2: I will save money at all costs.

Saving Money

Regarding money, are you a debtor, a spender, or a saver?

- Debtor – you spend more than you earn

- Spender – you spend all that you earn

- Saver – you save a portion of what you earn

Most people are debtors and spenders. It is easy to spend

money, but saving it is hard work. It takes patience, dedication, foresight, and sacrifice, but saving money is also the cornerstone of godly stewardship and wealth creation.

It also requires wisdom. The Bible reminds us of the wisdom of saving and planning for the future: *Precious treasure and oil are in a wise man's dwelling, but a foolish man devours it* (Proverbs 21:20). Wise people do not squander their resources. They make an intentional choice to save money at all costs. This is especially significant when you have a spouse, children, parents, or other dependents for whom you are responsible. Wisdom shows itself in careful planning.

Scripture gives us an example of financial wisdom in the story of Joseph. When Egypt faced seven years of famine, Joseph demonstrated his wisdom by advising Pharaoh of a savings plan to preserve Egypt and provide food for the world. In years of plentiful harvest, Joseph set aside resources because he looked ahead to years of famine. Egypt was prepared because Joseph was *discerning and wise*, guided by the Spirit of God (Genesis 41:39). He was a faithful steward who knew the value of saving over squandering and considered his responsibility to be of greater importance than his own convenience.

Whether you earn minimum wage or a six-figure salary, it is easy to overspend on nonessentials. Many people squander thousands of dollars a year on unnecessary spending – like specialty coffee drinks – making Starbucks' investors rich while they continue to live paycheck to paycheck. Wise people exercise self-restraint, knowing that every dollar spent is money they will never see again.

If you are ready to commit to this second decision, here are some valuable habits to begin cultivating in your life:

1. Keep track of your money.

This may sound simple, but it is profound. Your goal is to save money so that you can eventually invest it, but it is nearly impossible if you do not know how much you have and where it goes. To have a clear picture of your income and expenses, you must keep track of every penny that you earn and every penny that you spend.

The best way – or, arguably, the *only* way – to keep track of your money is to live within a budget. While some people hate the word *budget*, you can make it more exciting and less restrictive than you think. Think of it this way: You get to create and follow your own rules, deciding where and how you spend money.

Creating and following a budget will empower you to say no to unnecessary spending. If you are driven by emotion and circumstances, a budget will allow you to practice self-control and to resist the indulgence of the flesh. Holding yourself accountable to the budget allowances will be difficult, but it will yield positive results.

Six Foundational Steps to Creating a Budget

Creating a budget is a powerful first step to managing your finances. Follow these six steps to get started:

Step 1: Gather your regular bills, such as cell phone, internet, and utilities.

Step 2: Look at your receipts or checking and debit account statements to see how you spend your money. On a sheet of paper, create spending categories like entertainment, eating out, and transportation, and write down how much was spent in each category last month. Many banking apps will do this for you.

Step 3: Determine your monthly income. Review your pay stubs and all streams of income and add them together.

Step 4: Subtract your monthly expenses from your monthly income.

Step 5: Distinguish between money spent on needs and money spent on wants. Utilities are a need. Amazon Prime is a want. Write an N next to needs and a W next to wants.

Step 6: Now look for things you can reduce or eliminate to increase your available funds or extra money. Pay particular attention to your wants. Freeing up extra money allows you to:

- stop adding to your debt (We will cover debt in more detail later.)
- pay down the debt you already have

- place more money into savings (once you've paid down your debts)

- live frugally today so you can enjoy wealth tomorrow

Create Your Budget

Now look in the back of this book at *Resource 1: Budget Worksheet*. Fill in this sheet to get an estimate of your income and expenses for the following month. Carefully allocate funds to the appropriate categories, keeping your needs in mind. Your goal is to budget your money so that you put more money toward debt payments, savings, and investments, and less money toward your wants.

You will notice an *Unexpected Expenses* expenditure on the worksheet. This is an important budget item. You never know when your car will break down or your air conditioner will stop working. The Unexpected Expenses category will help you prepare for those inevitable, unplanned costs everyone incurs. Assign a realistic dollar amount for this category.

As you create your budget, keep the following three things in mind: First, set realistic expectations. A budget that is too restrictive or that fails to account for unexpected expenses can lead to frustration. When goals are unachievable, you will be more likely to abandon the plan altogether.

Second, make a firm commitment to the budget. Living off a budget requires consistent self-control to resist impulse spending or the temptation to make unnecessary "exceptions." Without discipline, even the best budget will fail.

Third, keep track of every dollar spent. If you do not, it will be difficult to stick to the budget. You will lose sight of where your money goes and can easily overspend without realizing it.

Keeping a close eye on your finances helps you make better decisions. Budgeting apps can help make this process easier by automatically tracking your spending and sending notifications when you approach category limits. Several popular budgeting apps, like Monarch Money and YNAB, offer features to link your bank accounts, track expenses, and set budget goals. Other apps to investigate include Goodbudget, NerdWallet, and PocketGuard.

Make sure your family and friends know you are on a budget and that you cannot and *will not* throw your money away. Do not be rude about it; simply say, "I am sorry we cannot go to California with you. We are on a budget."

2. Earn extra money.

If you intend to build wealth, it is beneficial to have multiple streams of income. Here are a few ways to earn extra money:

- Sell things online. Sell your unneeded and unused items on sites like Poshmark or Facebook Marketplace. Many items in your house or garage can be easily converted into cash.

- Start a side hustle. It is quite easy to start a side gig these days, thanks to the internet. Animal lovers can make money walking other people's dogs or pet sitting, and handy people can offer their services to those in their community. Some side hustles can be quite lucrative, so think about how you might turn your hobby into a moneymaking enterprise.

- Find a part-time job. Many types of jobs can help you earn extra income in your spare time. If you are skilled in a certain industry or occupation, those skills can be put to work to help you get ahead. You might consider driving for Uber or delivering food for places like Grubhub or Uber Eats. You may not consider this type of work to be your dream job, but it can help you meet your financial goals.

3. Pause before you purchase.

Impulse buying is one of the greatest threats to maintaining a savings habit. Train yourself to pause before making any purchase and ask three simple questions:

1. Can I really afford it?

2. Do I really need it?

3. Is it worth what I am paying for it?

In many cases, you will find that no is the correct answer to one or more of these questions. Asking them will help you think critically about your purchases.

4. Save and invest all salary increases.

When you receive a raise, it is tempting to expand your lifestyle. Instead, make a commitment to save and invest every salary increase. By doing this, you resist "lifestyle inflation" and ensure that your additional income builds your financial future. Imagine receiving a $5,000 annual raise. It might be tempting to spend that extra money each month, but choosing to invest it will significantly grow your wealth over time due to compound interest, which we will explore in Chapter 4. Proverbs 13:11 reminds us: *Whoever gathers [wealth] little by little will increase it.* Incremental savings can yield substantial results.

You should also invest any bonuses or tax refunds you receive. They may feel like "extra money," but they can be powerful opportunities to achieve your financial goals. Instead of splurging, which most people do, direct such windfalls into savings and investments. You can even direct them to fund your emergency savings or pay down debt. Do not squander your raises, bonuses, and tax refunds; instead, take advantage of them to multiply your blessings.

5. Eliminate unused subscriptions and invest the savings.

Unused subscriptions and memberships are silent drains on your finances. Take time to review all your recurring expenses, including streaming services, gym memberships, and apps, and cancel anything you are not using. Redirect that money into savings or investments. This habit embodies the principle Jesus spoke about: *"One who is faithful in a very little is also faithful in much"* (Luke 16:10). Being faithful with small amounts prepares you to manage larger sums wisely.

6. Take on tasks you normally pay others to do.
Many everyday services we pay for can be done ourselves with a little planning and effort. By taking on some of these tasks yourself, you can significantly reduce spending:

- Wash your own car rather than taking it to a car wash.

- Prepare meals at home rather than dining out or ordering takeout.

- If you eat out occasionally, do so at lunchtime, which can be half the cost of dinner.

- Walk, jog, and do workouts at home. This alone can save hundreds of dollars annually.

- Check out books from the library rather than purchasing them.

- Style your own hair.

- Drink filtered tap water rather than bottled water.

- Repair your clothing rather than replace it.

Doing things yourself takes time and energy, but think of it as paying yourself. The principle here is to be industrious and resourceful. The virtuous woman of Proverbs 31 models this well: *She looks well to the ways of her household and does not eat the bread of idleness* (Proverbs 31:27).

7. Set up automatic bank transfers into your savings.

One of the most effective ways to save money is to make it automatic. Set up a recurring transfer from your checking account to a savings or investment account. This "out of sight, out of mind" strategy ensures that you save consistently without having to think about it every month or rely on willpower.

8. Establish clear financial goals.

Setting clear financial goals is essential for wealth building and stewardship because it provides direction, focus, and motivation. Goals serve as a roadmap, helping you prioritize your resources and make intentional decisions that align with your values and vision. Without goals, financial planning can be reactive, leading to missed opportunities and poor resource management. *Resource 2: Financial Goals Workshop* will walk you through the process of establishing short-term, mid-term, and long-term goals.

We recommend that you invest the time to set goals and write them down. "It does not exist unless it is in writing" is a good rule of thumb, especially when it comes to goal setting. Write down your goals and display them in a visible location to keep them on your mind.

Even though they may be written down, keep in mind that goals are not set in stone. Circumstances change, and when they do, you may need to adjust your goals. Make the needed changes and keep moving forward. As you establish goals, include ones that relate to savings, potential streams of income investing (Chapter 4), getting out of debt (Chapter 5), and giving to the Lord's work (Chapter 6).

9. Stay committed to your plan.

It is easy to say we are going to do something, but much harder to follow through with it. Why do so many people give up on their New Year's resolution even during the first week of January? They take the path of least resistance because discipline is challenging, but you will not become wealthy unless you are fully committed to your plan.

If you want to take control of your life and your future, a halfhearted commitment will not be good enough. Stephen Covey, in his bestselling book *The 7 Habits of Highly Effective People,* explained that highly effective people make and keep commitments to themselves: "By making and keeping promises to ourselves and others, little by little, our honor becomes greater than our moods. The power to make and keep commitments to ourselves is the essence of developing the basic habits of effectiveness."[2]

Our honor must become greater than our moods and our feelings. Sometimes we can get in a spending mood because we feel good when we buy things. But

---

2   Stephen Covey, *The 7 Habits of Highly Effective People: Powerful Lessons in Personal Change* (New York: Simon & Schuster, 1989), 51.

when we make a commitment to doing something, like saving our money, our word needs to trump our whims.

Commit to saving your money – and stick to it! And if, on the rare occasion you overspend and veer from your budget, do not use this as an excuse to give up completely. Just rededicate yourself to the plan and keep going.

The Rewards of Saving at All Costs

The reason many people do not save their money is because they have wrong ideas about it. Some think they are too young to start saving: "I can save money later. I have lots of time." Others believe they waited too long and they are now too old: "It is too late to begin saving and investing money. I should have done it years ago." Still others say they are too broke: "I do not make enough to save. I am barely making it now." Many attitudes keep people stuck in a paycheck-to-paycheck mentality.

Saving money at all costs is not about deprivation; it is about stewardship, intentionality, and long-term blessings. It equips you to weather financial storms, provide for your family, and share generously with others. As you implement these savings habits, trust in God's provision and guidance. The Bible assures us: *My God will supply every need of yours according to his riches in glory in Christ Jesus* (Philippians 4:19). By being faithful stewards of what God has entrusted to us, we position ourselves to experience financial peace and abundance.

Do not take this second decision lightly. *I will save money at all costs* is a life-altering decision that demands courage and fortitude. But if you choose to make it, you will have taken another crucial step toward financial security and blessings.

Chapter 3

It Hurts, but the Pain Is Not in Vain

No person is free who is not master of himself.
– Epictetus

When you commit to saving money at all costs, you take action. You keep track of every dollar you earn and spend, set up financial goals for your future, and commit to fulfilling your savings plan.

But understand this: Your commitment will be tested. You will be tempted to spend money on things you really do not need. Our culture markets discontent as a way of life. Every advertisement is designed to stir desire – for a better car, a bigger house, a newer phone, or just a little more comfort. The constant message is clear: You need more to be happy. But the more we chase those desires, the more enslaved we become to them.

Scripture consistently teaches us that self-control is essential to faithful living. When we manage money according to our desires instead of God's design, we quickly lose sight of what really matters. But when we submit our desires to Christ, we find freedom and clarity. Godly stewardship requires mastering our desires, not letting them master us.

You have made two life-transforming decisions so far. This next one will require you to exert self-control and resist instant gratification.

DECISION 3: I will not let pleasure control me or distract me from faithfully stewarding God's resources.

Master Your Desires

We all must make this decision, and it is one that is just as difficult as it is essential. It is essential because without it, we will not build lasting wealth, but it is challenging because it wars against our flesh. Scripture tells us that *the desires of the flesh are against the Spirit, and the desires of the Spirit are against the flesh* (Galatians 5:17). This inner conflict often plays out in our spending habits.

King Solomon warned: *Whoever loves pleasure will be a poor man; he who loves wine and oil will not be rich* (Proverbs 21:17). That description fits many people today. Their relentless pursuit of *wine and oil,* things that bring pleasure, drains their bank accounts and controls their lives. They may earn a good income, but they quickly deplete their savings by buying things they enjoy, even seemingly harmless indulgences. For example, some people buy expensive coffee drinks daily. A couple who together spend $12 per day on such drinks are spending approximately $360 per month, which is more than $4,300 per year. Cutting back on coffee alone can help a couple be better stewards of God's resources and be able to put more money toward investments.

As you make the decision to master your desires, it will require determination and resolve. You will need to do at least three things:

1. Make sacrifices.

Saving money demands difficult sacrifices. These sacrifices challenge our desire for comfort and instant gratification but are necessary steps toward financial freedom. Sacrifice is essential because wealth is rarely an accident; it requires intentional planning and discipline. Here are some sacrifices that may be necessary if you are to reach your financial goals:

- Reduce discretionary spending. This might mean cutting back on such things as entertainment subscriptions and streaming services.

- Eat out less. Have your friends over for a barbeque rather than spending your hard-earned money at a restaurant. Make wise grocery purchases to prepare your own meals. You will not only save money, but you also most likely will eat healthier.

- Give up expensive coffee drinks. You can easily make your favorite drinks at home and save money.

- Be frugal when shopping for necessities. Stay away from expensive brand-name items when the generic brand will work the same. Look for sales, coupons, and online discounts. The extra effort will pay off in savings made.

- Stop buying new. Consignment clothing stores sell gently used clothing, and you can find just about any used product online for half the cost or less. But even with used items, only buy them if you truly need them.

- Downsize lifestyle choices. Moving to a smaller home, driving an older car, and eliminating nonessential memberships or clubs are common ways to save.

This decision will involve making many sacrifices. Only you know what your wine and olive oil are. Take time to think about what you really need; it is vital to distinguish between what is essential and what is merely a desire.

It is normal to dread the thought of having to give up some pleasures. Making sacrifices is difficult because it runs counter to human nature. Our culture values comfort, instant gratification, and social status. We feel the urge to keep up with our neighbors, even if we cannot afford to. Sacrifice requires us to say no to ourselves, a discipline that usually feels unpleasant and even painful at times, but it is necessary to prevent spiritual and financial breakdown.

Joseph is an example of someone who was presented

with and resisted the temptation of immediate gratification in various life circumstances. He could have
indulged in sexual pleasure with his master's wife, but
he resisted the urge because of his conscience before
God (Genesis 39:7-9). When he was summoned before
Pharaoh to interpret his dream, Joseph could have
taken advantage of the encounter and negotiated terms
for his release from prison before giving Pharaoh the
interpretation (Genesis 41:14-40).

That would have been self-satisfying and self-pre-
serving, especially since he did not owe any allegiance
to his foreign captors. Instead, he denied himself the
opportunity for self-promotion and let God work out
the details of exalting him to a high position of authority. In making these difficult sacrifices – denying what
seemed lucrative to the flesh and sensible to the natural mind – Joseph saved his righteous reputation and
preserved his relationship with the Lord.

His restraint applied to financial stewardship as well.
He led the entire nation of Egypt to set aside substantial
portions of grain during the seven years of abundance,
and we see how their sacrifice yielded dividends during
the seven years of famine that ensued (Genesis 41:47-49).
Joseph and the Egyptians took control of their futures by
giving up the short-term pleasure of plentiful eating. God
honored their stewardship: *There was famine in all lands,
but in all the land of Egypt there was bread* (Genesis 41:54).

God's Word is filled with examples of sacrifice that
yield long-term blessings. The things we give up or
resist for the purpose of saving money are not losses

but investments, allowing us to rightly steward our resources and prepare to care for others.

Making sacrifices to save money is difficult but vital for achieving financial freedom. By surrendering short-term pleasures, we prepare for long-term stability and honor God as faithful stewards. This self-denial is part of disciplining the flesh, which promotes spiritual character.

As we embrace discipline and learn to trust in God's provision, we find that sacrifices do more than build financial security. They deepen our faith and lead to spiritual growth and fulfillment.

2. Defer gratification.

When you refuse to let pleasure control your decisions and your destiny, you give up some good things today so you can experience a better life later. We call this concept *delayed gratification*. It is a hard concept for many of us to grasp – and even harder to live out. When we want something, we feel that we must have it right now. We are programmed for instant gratification.

Saving money may require you to defer gratification for a while. The key is to stay focused, not on temporary pleasures but on what will truly enhance your future.

In *The Psychology of Money*, Morgan Housel tells the story of Ronald Read, a man who spent decades pumping gas and working as a janitor. When he died, his estate was worth more than $8 million.[3]

Read had no college degree, no formal experience, and no connections. But he saved his money, putting

---

3   Morgan Housel, *The Psychology of Money: Timeless Lessons on Wealth, Greed, and Happiness* (Petersfield, UK: Harriman House, 2020), 2-3.

every spare penny into stocks that he held onto for decades. Read is a man whose children could say, *House and wealth are inherited from fathers* (Proverbs 19:14).

Read became wealthy because he knew how to defer gratification. He did not get caught up in wine and olive oil. He held on to old-fashioned virtues like "A penny saved is a penny earned." It is through timeless virtues that true greatness is built.

The book of Hebrews gives us many examples of faithful believers who died *not having received the things promised, but having seen them and greeted them from afar* (Hebrews 11:13). The story of faith is one of delayed gratification. Faith believes that the value of what is to come outweighs whatever is here and now. Through the eyes of patient faith, these Old Testament saints desired *a better country, that is, a heavenly one* (Hebrews 11:16), and traded what they had for what God had promised.

Delaying gratification requires patience. Progress may be slow, and you might be tempted to give up when you do not see dramatic increases in your savings balance. You may even ask if all this sacrifice is really worth it. It is. If you could ask Mr. Read, he would tell you the sacrifice is *definitely* worth it, but it takes time. You must be willing to wait and patiently nurture the mindset that not every desire must be immediately fulfilled.

3. Change your perspective on contentment.
Sacrificing and delaying gratification become especially hard if we think we will find contentment in what we

own. Scripture teaches that true satisfaction does not come from possessions but from a relationship with God.

Moses refused both the pleasures of sin and treasures of wealth in Egypt in order to be *mistreated with the people of God* and bear *the reproach of Christ* (Hebrews 11:24, 26). The knowledge of God held greater power than the throne of a worldly empire, and Moses found satisfying purpose in obeying God's call.

The apostle Paul knew where satisfaction and contentment come from. He wrote: *I have learned, in whatever situation I am, to be content. I know how to be brought low, and I know how to abound. In any and every circumstance, I have learned the secret of facing plenty and hunger, abundance and need. I can do all things through him who strengthens me* (Philippians 4:11-13). This perspective shifts the focus from earthly wealth to eternal treasures, reminding us that our ultimate security and joy are found in Christ, not in money or possessions.

Because Paul was confident that Christ would supply his needs, he had found *the secret* to being content: full reliance on God. If we, too, adopt this perspective, we can be content with what we have and free from control by pleasures.

It is not a sin to enjoy the pleasures of life, but it is a sin to be enslaved or enticed by them. Live *free from love of money, and be content with what you have, for he has said, "I will never leave you nor forsake you"* (Hebrews 13:5).

Christ is all we need and is always there to provide. If He is your true treasure, you may have nothing else, yet possess everything (2 Corinthians 6:10).

A Difficult but Rewarding Decision

We have challenged you in this chapter to make a very important decision: *I will not let pleasure control me or distract me from faithfully stewarding God's resources.*

This commitment will not be easy, but it will be worth it. You are giving up short-term pleasures and conveniences to achieve long-term goals. Making this decision puts you in position to take control of your future by not allowing your pleasures to control you.

Before moving on to the next chapter, take a few moments to answer the following questions. Your answers will help you stay committed to the wealth-building process.

1. What luxuries or non-essentials will you need to give up so that you can stay aligned with your financial goals and savings plan?

   List both the obvious and not-so-obvious sacrifices you will need to make. (If you have not yet set clear financial goals, be sure to complete the worksheets provided in *Resource 1* and *Resource 2*.)

2. What challenges or obstacles might hinder you from making the above sacrifices? These obstacles might include mindsets, personal obligations, habits, or aspects of your current lifestyle. Be specific.

3. What strategies will you use to overcome these obstacles?

Chapter 4

Every Dollar Compounds

My wealth has come from a combination of living in America, some lucky genes, and compound interest.
– Warren Buffett

In the first three chapters of this book, we have challenged you to make some calculated decisions. These decisions require you to:

- view money as a tool, not a treasure

- save money diligently and intentionally – at all costs

- exert self-control and discipline as part of your commitment to build wealth and steward your resources

If you have committed to these decisions and followed through, you will have already allocated money for savings. Now that you have saved money, what should you do with it? We are called to invest these resources wisely, prayerfully, and intentionally, using money to grow opportunity and create lasting impact. God expects a return on what He entrusts to us; He expects us to multiply it.

The principle of multiplication is woven throughout Scripture. God's command to us to be fruitful, Jesus feeding the multitudes, and the early church's explosive growth all demonstrate multiplication. Financial stewardship echoes this divine pattern. A wise steward grows what he is given so that it may bless others and glorify God.

If you are ready to multiply what God has entrusted to you, it is time for another decision.

DECISION 4: I will invest the resources God has entrusted to me and let every dollar multiply.

Imagine receiving a gift with a note that says, "Use this wisely." There is a weight that comes with that kind of responsibility. In much the same way, God entrusts us with resources – our time, talent, and treasure – and He expects us to not waste or hoard them but to invest them meaningfully.

In the parable of the minas, Jesus told of a man of noble birth who was about to go to a distant country to be appointed king and then return. He called his servants and gave them one mina, which equaled about four months wages for the average worker. The nobleman told them, *"Engage in business until I come"* (Luke 19:13).

When the nobleman returned, one of the servants earned 1,000 percent, saying, *"Lord, your mina has made ten minas more"* (Luke 19:16). The nobleman rewarded him and said, *"Because you have been faithful in a very little, you shall have authority over ten cities"* (Luke 19:17). Another servant had made five minas and was given authority over five cities. But then we read of the servant who did not invest the money. He said, *"Lord, here is your mina, which I kept laid away in a handkerchief"* (Luke 19:20). The nobleman harshly rebuked this servant because he failed to invest what he was given. At the very least, he could have put it in the bank to earn interest (Luke 19:23).

The nobleman represents Jesus, who has gone away to receive a kingdom and will one day return to reward His servants – us. Though He is not physically present with us now, He will come again at a future date and assess how we managed what He entrusted us with.

This parable has various applications to steward-ship, especially concerning the truth of the gospel. Each servant was given the same amount, one mina, and expected to invest it and present the results to the lord on his return. It is the mina that does the work, not the servant, and each servant acknowledged that the mina belonged to the lord – *"Your mina has made. . ."* (Luke 19:16, 18). However, the servants were character-ized by their wisdom or foolishness in their investment decisions. They were not judged by how much they had received but by what they had done with it.

We who have received the good news of the gospel have a responsibility to evangelize (invest) and allow the message of God's salvation through Jesus Christ to bear fruit (profit). Unfortunately, some who are ashamed of the message or who have a wrong view of Christ are like the third servant who failed in his investment. Though he possessed a valuable treasure, he foolishly kept it hidden rather than let it work and grow.

Paul exhorts Timothy in a similar way about *the stewardship from God that is by faith* (1 Timothy 1:4). Regarding the gospel, Paul considers believers the stewards of this *good deposit* of truth that leads to salvation (2 Timothy 1:14). To invest it properly before the King returns, we must *preach the word* (2 Timothy 4:2).

In Jesus' parable, He uses money as an object lesson for the principles of good stewardship – principles that apply to all areas of life. God entrusts us with our lives, and all our resources should be used to build His kingdom. This begins with our response to and use of the gospel, but it also extends to how we invest the resources He has given us. One day we will give an account to the Lord for how we handled both spiritual truth and material resources.

The parable of the talents (Matthew 25:14-30) makes a similar point, but the amounts to be invested are much, much larger. A talent was a unit of money valued at 6,000 drachmas, the equivalent of about twenty years' wages for a laborer. In approximate modern-day equivalents, if a laborer works 2,000 hours a year at $20 per hour, he will earn $40,000 per year. So, a talent today would be equivalent to about $800,000. In this parable, though, each servant was given a *different* number of talents.

One man was given five talents to invest, another two, and another one. The one who had five talents made five talents more. The one with two talents also doubled the money. But the one with one talent buried the money in the ground and hid it. Jesus commends the servants who invested the money, saying, *"Well done, good and faithful servant. You have been faithful over a little; I will set you over much. Enter into the joy of your master"* (Matthew 25:21, 23). It is clear that the commendation is based on faithfulness and effort, not on the size of the result. Both faithful servants made 100 percent on their investments even though they had different resource amounts.

But the master called the one who buried the money a *wicked and slothful servant* (Matthew 25:26). The master told him, *"You ought to have invested my money with the bankers, and at my coming I should have received what was my own with interest"* (Matthew 25:27). The servant was a foolish investor because he was lazy and did not put his deposit to work. He spent his time and energy digging a hole rather than wisely managing his talent.

These talents could represent our various spiritual gifts, abilities, monetary resources, and opportunities, but no matter the spiritual application you make, the lesson we learn in both parables is this: We must be faithful servants of all that God has entrusted to our care. The faithful servants in the parables made the decision to invest the money that had been entrusted to them so that it could multiply. God wants us to manage His resources wisely, increase them, and use them for His purposes.

The work of the faithful servants was worth it because God blessed them for their stewardship. They were able to enter into the joy of their master and were rewarded with additional opportunities to serve God faithfully: *"For to everyone who has will more be given, and he will have an abundance"* (Matthew 25:29; see also Luke 19:26).

Making Investments

As you commit to stewarding the money God has entrusted to you, there are several ways to grow it. Let us look at these options, including some of the various pros and cons of diverse investments. We will begin with a basic savings account and then discuss more aggressive ways to multiply your resources.

1. Regular Savings Account

A savings account is a cornerstone of personal finance, offering a safe, easily accessible place to store funds while earning modest interest. The key benefits are security, liquidity, and simplicity. Savings accounts in the United States are FDIC-insured up to $250,000 per depositor, funds can be accessed quickly, and they are easy to open and manage, with no complex terms or requirements.

But you will not grow wealth with a savings account alone. The low interest rates are usually below inflation, which means the value of money can erode over time. Having funds available in a savings account is important since it allows you to access your money when needed, but the following options will allow you to grow your savings faster.

2. Certificate of Deposit

Certificates of Deposit (CDs) are time deposits where you commit funds for a fixed period in exchange for a higher interest rate than regular savings accounts. CDs are opened through a bank or credit union for a specific length of time, such as six months, one year, or five years. While CDs are FDIC-insured and offer higher interest rates than savings accounts, you will be penalized for early withdrawal.

3. Money Market Funds

Money market funds (MMFs) are mutual funds that invest in low-risk, short-term debt instruments like treasury bills. As mutual funds, they pool money from multiple investors to invest in a diversified portfolio managed by professionals. MMFs are opened through a mutual fund provider or a brokerage. Because they have professional management and diversification, they do have higher potential returns than savings accounts, but the returns depend on interest rate environments.

4. US Treasury Bills

US Treasury bills (T-bills) are short-term government securities that are sold at a discount and mature at face value. T-bills, which are purchased directly through Treasury Direct or a brokerage, are backed by the US government and are virtually risk free. They are also exempt from state and local taxes. However, they historically offer lower returns than stocks or mutual funds and have limited growth potential for long-term investors.

5. Stock Mutual Funds

These funds use pooled investor money to purchase a diversified portfolio of stocks, aiming for long-term growth. You can invest in a stock market fund through a brokerage account or directly with mutual fund companies like Fidelity or Vanguard. The pros include higher potential returns than fixed-income investments and professional management and diversification, but there are cons to consider: Market volatility can lead to losses, and fees and expense ratios reduce returns.

6. Exchange-Traded Funds

Exchange-Traded Funds (ETFs), which are purchased through brokerage accounts, are investment funds that trade on stock exchanges and hold a mix of assets such as stocks, bonds, and commodities. When you buy ETFs, your portfolio will hold a variety of companies and industries. The advantage is that if one company performs poorly, it will not ruin your portfolio because other companies may be performing well. Like stocks, ETFs are easy to trade, but also like stocks, prices do fluctuate.

7. Individual Stocks and Bonds

Investing directly in stocks and bonds allows you to tailor your portfolio to your preferences. Stocks are a type of security representing ownership in a company, entitling the holder to a share of the company's profits and assets. (See *Exhibit 1: Crash Course on the Stock Market* for a discussion on how the stock market works.)

A bond is a fixed-income investment. It is a debt security issued by the government or a corporation in exchange for money you lend them with regular interest payments.

Stocks can provide high returns but carry high risk based on market volatility. Bonds offer steady income and lower risk, but they offer lower returns. You can purchase stocks and bonds through an online brokerage or a financial advisor.

8. Cryptocurrency

Digital currencies like Bitcoin and Ethereum offer decentralized alternatives to traditional currencies. You can open an account on a cryptocurrency exchange, such as Coinbase or Binance, and purchase digital assets. While cryptocurrency offers the potential for high returns, it carries extreme volatility and risk of loss. There is also a lack of regulation and potential for scams. To see how these investment options compare to a savings account, see below:

As you consider investment options, consider your goals and time horizon: Savings accounts and CDs are good for short-term goals, while mutual funds, ETFs, and stocks are more suitable for long-term growth. Also consider your risk tolerance. Conservative investors may prefer T-bills or money market funds, while risk-tolerant investors might explore stocks or cryptocurrency.

Finally, be sure to diversify. Combining multiple investment types can balance risk and return. While a savings account is valuable for accessibility and stability, diversifying into higher-yield options can significantly enhance the growth of savings over time. Each option has its place, depending on your financial goals, time horizon, and risk appetite.

Exponential Growth

How much should you invest? It all depends on your goals, of course, but generally, you should invest as much as you can. The more you invest, the more you will make as your money grows exponentially. A good option is to commit a fixed dollar amount from each paycheck to invest. You can determine this amount from the budget you made in Chapter 2.

Warren Buffett, the retired chairman of Berkshire Hathaway, has amassed a net worth of over $154 billion dollars (as of 2025). His path to wealth began at a young age when he started investing in the stock market after learning about the power of compound interest.

In Alice Schroeder's biography of Buffett, *The Snowball,* she explains that Buffett learned about compound interest when he was just ten years old. He had read a book that illustrated how $1,000 could turn into a fortune. He learned that $1,000 earning 10 percent interest would be worth:

- $1,600 in 5 years
- $2,600 in 10 years
- $10,800 in 25 years
- $117,400 in 50 years

Schroeder said that Buffett "could picture the numbers compounding as vividly as the way a snowball grew when he rolled it across the lawn." As soon as Buffett learned about compound interest, he began to think differently about money. "If a dollar today was going to be worth ten some years from now, then in his mind the two were the same."[4] The young Buffett would say things like, "Do I really want to spend $300,000 for this haircut?" To Buffett, a few dollars spent were wasted because those few dollars could not compound. Schroeder wrote that when Buffett bought his house in Omaha for $31,500 in his late twenties, he called it "Buffett's Folly," for "in his mind, $31,500 was a million dollars after compounding."[5]

How Compound Interest Works

Compound interest is simply earning interest on your investment and on the interest your investment earned. The longer your money is invested, the more time it has to compound. Buffett calls this principle the "Methuselah Technique" after the oldest man recorded in the Bible (Genesis 5:27). According to the Methuselah Technique, building wealth is not just about how much the money you invest grows but also how *long* it grows. The more time you give your money, the more it can multiply.

Imagine a young person investing $2,000 per year for eight years. His total investment would be worth $16,000. Keeping in mind that a 12 percent return is considered aggressive growth and comes with much risk, here is what his investment would look like over a span of 40 years at a 12 percent interest rate:

---

4   Alice Schroeder, *The Snowball: Warren Buffett and the Business of Life* (New York: Bantam Books, 2009), 60-61.

5   Schroeder, *The Snowball*, 187-188.

YEAR	INVESTMENT	BALANCE
1	2,000	2,240
2	2,000	4,749
3	2,000	7,558
4	2,000	10,706
5	2,000	14,230
6	2,000	18,178
7	2,000	22,599
8	2,000	27,551
9	0	30,857
10	0	34,560
11	0	38,708
12	0	43,352
13	0	48,554
14	0	54,381
15	0	60,907
16	0	68,216
17	0	76,802
18	0	85,570
19	0	95,383
20	0	107,339
21	0	120,220
22	0	134,646
23	0	150,804
24	0	168,900
25	0	189,168
26	0	211,869
27	0	237,293
28	0	265,768
29	0	297,660
30	0	333,385
31	0	373,385
32	0	418,191
33	0	468,374
34	0	524,579
35	0	587,528
36	0	658,032
37	0	736,995
38	0	825,435
39	0	924,487
40	0	1,035,425

That young person, with just a $16,000 investment, and assuming a 12% annual return, would have more than $1,000,000 available when he is older. Now imagine if he dedicates much more per year and stays committed to that investment strategy over the span of his life. He will amass great wealth.

The Methuselah Technique does not play favorites. It is a principle rooted in time and discipline, and it works whether you earn minimum wage or a six-figure income. With patience and self-control, even small investments can yield great wealth. And, of course, with larger investments, you will enjoy larger dividends.

Before making a purchase, consider what you could accomplish with that money if it were to grow for decades. You might be tempted, for example, to buy the latest and greatest cell phone for $1,000. But in essence, with compound interest, you may be missing out on a $117,400 investment. If you begin to look at your purchases through a compound interest lens, you will be less likely to spend that money and more likely to invest it for your future.

Getting Started for New Investors with a Small Initial Investment

There are many online brokers today that will allow you to open an account with no minimum requirements. Historically, one had to have a small sum of money (e.g., $2,500) to open an account with a brokerage firm. Today, you can open an account with as little as $50.

There are many online trading platforms that make it easy to invest, such as Betterment (www.betterment.

com) and Robinhood (www.robinhood.com). This is not an endorsement of these companies but merely an example of the types of companies that allow new investors to get started with a minimal investment. Obviously, as your account grows and your wealth increases, you will want to consider if having a financial advisor makes more sense to you than tackling it alone.

Setting Up an Account

Creating an account with an online investment company is simple, and most companies offer apps that enable you to set up accounts and make transactions on your phone, tablet, or computer.

You can choose from several types of accounts, including individual taxable accounts, Roth IRAs, traditional IRAs, and even trust accounts, depending on your goals and how much risk you are willing to take.

Selecting a Portfolio

When you invest in an online trading company, you have the option to purchase individual company stocks or invest in a diversified portfolio of low-cost exchange-traded funds (ETFs).

The problem with investing in only one company or industry is the risk of putting all your eggs in one basket. Your investment can take a big hit if the company underperforms or goes bankrupt. King Solomon said, *Give a portion to seven, or even to eight, for you know not what disaster may happen on earth* (Ecclesiastes 11:2).

Diversifying your investments helps protect you from unexpected disasters by spreading your money across various investments.

When you invest in an ETF, you can make transactions in exact dollar amounts (e.g., $25). You will not be able to select a particular company to invest in, but you will be able to set your desired level of risk. Based on your stated risk level, the online company will recommend a portfolio and will manage buying and selling funds for you in that portfolio.

Investing Ethically

When you begin your investment journey, your natural goal is to see your money grow. But as a Christian, wise investing means more than financial profit. It also means honoring God with your resources. Not every profitable opportunity aligns with godly stewardship. Some companies may offer strong returns while simultaneously supporting practices or values that run contrary to your Christian convictions.

Every believer in Christ should consider investment ethics when investing money in the stock market. Since our investments supply money to publicly traded companies, knowing their policies and products beforehand can help us make informed decisions.

The Bible calls us to honor God with our wealth (Proverbs 3:9), and that includes choosing investments that promote biblical principles and refraining from investing in companies that promote immoral and anti-Christian activities, even if those companies are profitable. Believers should aim to align their investments with their spiritual and moral values, for example, avoiding companies that support abortion, adult entertainment, gambling, recreational drugs, LGBTQ+ activism (e.g., companies promoting agendas contrary to biblical marriage and sexuality), human rights abuses, and other blatantly unethical behaviors.

While our purpose in this chapter is not to single out individual companies, mentioning a few of them and their activities will help you understand some of the ethical dilemmas you will face when choosing to invest with godly wisdom. Here are examples of companies that engage in behaviors that run contrary to conservative Christian values:

MAC Cosmetics, owned by Estée Lauder Companies, has contributed over $2 million to organizations like Planned Parenthood and LGBTQ+ events and advocacy.

In 2016, Target issued a statement encouraging employees and customers to use restrooms and fitting rooms corresponding to their "gender identity," which may not correspond to their biological gender. This policy was part of Target's broader commitment to inclusivity and support for LGBTQ+ rights, which conflict with traditional Christian values.

Sometimes a company's actions are not easy to assess. Amazon has publicly committed to cover travel expenses for employees seeking abortions, but in 2024, it donated $150,000 to the Republican Attorneys General Association, which supported a candidate advocating for a total abortion ban. This donation has been viewed as contradictory to Amazon's stated pro-choice platform.

Every investor is accountable to God for the way in which he has stewarded the resources He has given. These sometimes-complex decisions require spiritual discernment and moral conscience based on God's Word.

Scripture offers us several tragic examples of people who failed to uphold moral standards, resulting in immoral endeavors and drastic consequences. When the Israelites entered the promised land, God commanded them to drive out all the Canaanites lest they covet their riches or be ensnared by their idolatrous practices (Deuteronomy 7:1-26). The Israelites did not obey. They thought it economically advantageous to put the Canaanites to forced labor rather than expel them. This disobedience was a catalyst of continual problems throughout their history (Judges 1:28-2:5).

Godly King Jehoshaphat made an alliance with Ahab and Ahaziah, evil kings of Israel, hoping for economic and military strength, but God made His wrath evident when He destroyed Jehoshaphat's shipping investment (2 Chronicles 20:31-37). Later, the Jews of Jerusalem tried to profit from business conducted on the Sabbath, completely disregarding God's Law. They may have evoked severe consequences from God had Nehemiah not intervened, emphasizing that God is a better source of blessing than business that violates His Word (Nehemiah 13:15-22).

Habakkuk rebuked those who developed cities with no regard for justice or the humane treatment of others. He said, *"Woe to him who builds a town with blood and founds a city on iniquity!"* (Habakkuk 2:12). This is a strong warning against profiting from injustice. While

Scripture does not specifically address this issue, we must be careful not to invest in companies and industries explicitly engaged in unethical practices and immorality.

Finally, the apostle Paul cautioned believers about locking themselves into personal and business relationships with unbelievers, a principle that can be applied to making financial investments. He said, *Do not be unequally yoked with unbelievers. For what partnership has righteousness with lawlessness? Or what fellowship has light with darkness?* (2 Corinthians 6:14). While not directly about investing, Paul's teaching calls us to be mindful about partnerships, including financial ones. We strongly encourage you not to be yoked with companies that oppose biblical values and gospel living.

The Challenge of Finding Suitable Investments

As Christians looking to invest in a way that aligns with our moral and biblical convictions, we face a significant challenge: No company is entirely "clean." If we scrutinize any business deeply enough, we will likely uncover practices, partnerships, proprietors, or policies that conflict with biblical values. Even companies that seem neutral on the surface may be indirectly tied to questionable activities through supply chains, labor practices, corporate donations, or marketing strategies.

Some industries generally perceived as neutral include:

- Technology – software companies, hardware manufacturers, and internet services

- Consumer Goods – companies producing food, clothing, and household items

- Transportation – airlines, logistics, and automotive companies

- Industrial Manufacturing – construction, engineering, equipment, and production

While these industries may not be inherently immoral, some businesses within them may engage in practices that conflict with Christian principles, such as supporting unethical labor conditions, promoting agendas contrary to biblical values, or engaging in deceptive business tactics.

We must also wrestle with our own convictions and contradictions. Every believer will face moments when their convictions are challenged by the complexities of the modern economy. One example from my own life (D. J.) illustrates this struggle.

Years ago, I invested in Phillip Morris, a leading producer of tobacco products, but I soon felt convicted about it. Tobacco is a major cause of cancer, heart disease, and various other health problems, and the undeniable harm caused by tobacco led me to question whether or not I should profit from something so destructive.

However, this conviction raised a deeper question: Where do I draw the line? One of my favorite historical figures and theological inspirations is Charles Spurgeon, a nineteenth-century preacher known for his passionate sermons and deep biblical insight. Spurgeon was also an occasional cigar smoker and defended the practice when criticized. Though I revere his teachings and faithfulness to Christ, I find myself at odds with his stance on smoking.

This presents an important dilemma: How do we reconcile admiration for someone's faith and wisdom with our disagreement with aspects of their personal choices? The same question applies to investing. If we choose not to invest in one industry due to moral concerns, does that mean we must scrutinize every company we engage with to the same degree? At what point does this become an impossible standard?

Navigating the Tension

The reality is that we live in a fallen world, and absolute purity in investing or in any economic engagement is challenging at best and unattainable at worst. While we should strive to honor God with our financial choices, we must also acknowledge the complexity of modern business. The key is to establish clear principles and apply them consistently while allowing room for grace and wisdom.

For me, questioning my investments in the tobacco industry was based on its direct and undeniable harm. I also try to avoid companies and industries that blatantly violate God's Word and harm God's people. Others may draw their own lines, refusing to profit from industries they believe are unethical or choosing to avoid companies that fund certain political or social causes or that exploit workers. Some Christians may even choose broader market index funds, reasoning that they are investing in the economy as a whole rather than endorsing every company within it.

Yet if you are a typical, simple investor who is working to pay the bills and trying to put some money away for retirement in an IRA or 401(k), you may not have the time or ability to investigate every company tied to your investment portfolio vehicles. Plus, getting too obsessive about drawing moral lines can make you more frantic and fanatical than faithful and frugal. Be wise, careful, but reasonable. Ultimately, each believer must seek the Lord's guidance, study Scripture, and make investment decisions with prayer in good conscience. The goal is not legalistic perfection but faithfulness to God in all areas of life, including finances.

The following discussion will help you create guidelines for investing that respect your biblical beliefs and convictions.

Biblically Responsible Investing

Biblically Responsible Investing (BRI) is an investment approach that aligns financial decisions with Christian values, helping to ensure that investments honor God and support ethical, faith-based principles. While it is impossible to guarantee that companies are 100 percent ethically conscientious, we feel that believers, to the best of their knowledge, should support companies that promote family values and ethical business practices, uphold biblical principles in their leadership and operations, demonstrate fairness in the way they treat employees and customers, and engage in charitable and faith-based initiatives.

As you create your portfolio, you can use faith-based investment screeners, such as Inspire Insight (inspireinsight.com), to help you. Inspire Insight filters companies based on Christian values. It is a free, online tool that provides access to biblical values data on more than 24,000 stocks, mutual funds, and ETFs.

Other online screeners include Timothy Plans Fund (timothyplan.com) and Eventide Funds (eventidefunds.com). Such tools can help you find companies that do not explicitly engage in immoral conduct. We say "explicitly" because the lifestyles, ethical behaviors, and faith of the board members and executive officers of these companies are, in most cases, not publicized.

If investing directly in individual stocks, it is beneficial to research specific companies. Investigate the company's policies, political donations, and corporate values, all of which will help you understand their corporate character. Websites like Morningstar, Yahoo Finance, and investor relations pages provide useful insights. For mutual funds and ETFs, review the fund's holdings to ensure they align with your values.

Investing in commodities like gold and silver can be compatible with biblically responsible investing, as these assets are generally considered morally neutral. However, it is essential to approach such investments with caution and wisdom, ensuring they serve as part of a diversified and prudent investment strategy. Consider a mix of asset classes, including BRI-compliant mutual funds, ETFs, and, if appropriate, commodities like gold and silver, ensuring a balanced and diversified portfolio.

It is also helpful to consult with a wealth manager or financial advisor, especially one experienced in BRI. A financial advisor can work with you to tailor an investment strategy that aligns with your beliefs and financial goals.

Most importantly, pray for wisdom and discernment. As believers, we are to seek God's wisdom in all decisions (Proverbs 3:5-6). Ask for discernment in selecting investments that honor God and align with your values. Before you begin to invest, we suggest that you carefully and prayerfully create your own guidelines as to what you will and will not invest in based on your spiritual convictions. Remember, your investment goals should be rooted in God's kingdom, not yours. This perspective will help you make decisions guided by your faith and values, reinforcing godly stewardship.

Advice for New Investors

As we close this chapter, I want to share the same advice I have given to new investors for over thirty-five years. In helping people manage and grow their wealth, I have seen how these principles can lead to lasting success for those who seek to steward the resources God has entrusted to them. The following reflects much of what we have discussed in this book, and I hope you carefully review the suggestions below as you begin your investing journey:

1. Define your financial goals.

Investing without clear goals is like sailing without a destination. Defining your goals – whether for retirement, buying a home, or building wealth for your family – gives purpose to your investment strategy. It is vital to write down both your short-term and long-term objectives. (See *Resource 2*.) Quantify them if possible (e.g., $60,000 for a down payment in five years). Remember that your financial goals must align with your spiritual responsibilities as a steward of God's resources. Let your financial goals also leave a spiritual inheritance for your family, church, and God's kingdom.

2. Determine your risk tolerance.

Your willingness to endure market fluctuations determines your comfort with different investment types. Assess your emotional and financial capacity to handle risk. Younger investors with a long horizon can typically afford to take more risks, while those closer to retirement may prefer safer options.

3. Start early and take advantage of compounding.

The earlier you start, the more time your investments have to grow due to compound interest. Even small, regular contributions can result in substantial growth over time.

4. Diversify your investments.

Diversification reduces risk by spreading investments across different asset classes, industries, and geographic regions. It is important to build a balanced portfolio that includes stocks, bonds, mutual funds, ETFs, and alternative investments. Such diversification is vital, for if tech stocks drop in value, for example, holding other stocks or bond investments might cushion your losses.

5. Focus on long-term growth, not short-term gains.

Emotional reactions to market fluctuations can easily lead to poor decisions, like panic selling or impulse buying. A well-known saying is true here: "Time in the market is more important than timing the market." Stay the course and avoid making impulsive decisions based on fear or greed. Remember, the stock market has historically trended upward over time. As you focus on long-term growth, your desire for profitable investment cannot contradict your accountability as a believer who claims to have the fruit of the Spirit – faith, patience, and self-control. God will not honor even the shrewdest investment strategies at the expense of Christian character.

6. Maintain an emergency fund.

Investing should never come at the expense of financial security. Unexpected expenses can force you to liquidate investments prematurely, potentially at a loss. It is wise to keep 6-12 months' worth of living expenses in a savings account or another liquid, low-risk option in case of job loss or emergencies. As a rule, only invest money you will not need in the short term.

7. Monitor and rebalance your portfolio.

Over time, market fluctuations can cause your portfolio

to drift from its target allocation, increasing your risk exposure. Periodically review your portfolio and rebalance it, if necessary, to align with your original strategy. For example, if your target allocation is 70 percent stocks and 30 percent bonds, a bull market may shift it to 80 percent stocks. Rebalancing restores stability and mitigates risk.

8. Work with a trusted advisor.

A qualified wealth manager can help you navigate financial decisions, tailor strategies to your goals, provide accountability, and help ensure that your financial decisions align with your Christian values. Regularly review your progress with your advisor and adjust strategies as your goals or life circumstances change.

9. Stay committed to your savings and investment plan.

Make a commitment and do not allow anything to steer you off course. Solomon said, *The plans of the diligent lead surely to abundance* (Proverbs 21:5). Notice the word *surely*. If you are diligent and stay committed to your savings and investment plan, you will be successful. If you are hasty and impetuous, you run a greater risk of loss: *Everyone who is hasty comes only to poverty* (Proverbs 21:5). Following these principles will help you build a portfolio that grows sustainably while aligning with your life goals.

In closing, as you invest and make every dollar multiply, you need to be patient and steadfast. Because new investors tend to check their portfolio accounts every day, they are often frustrated by what might seem to be slow growth. Do not allow that frustration to lead you to discontentment and poor decisions. Be patient. Good investing is boring. Keep an eye on your investment, add to it, and let it grow over time.

Remember to surrender everything to the Lord in prayer. If your investments steal away your peace and dependence on God, then your priorities are out of order. If you are unsettled with stress, impatience, worry, anxiety, greed, or obsession, then the enemy is defeating you emotionally and spiritually despite the results of your investments. God will not honor that. Money can be a lucrative blessing or a devastating curse. *Trust in the Lord, and do good. Delight yourself in the Lord, and he will give you the desires of your heart. Commit your way to the Lord; trust in him, and he will act. . . . Better is the little that the righteous has than the abundance of many wicked* (Psalm 37:3-5, 16).

As you make this fourth decision, *I will invest the resources God has entrusted to me and let every dollar multiply*, do not be like the servant who buried his money in the ground. Be a careful and diligent steward, *making the best use of the time* (Ephesians 5:16) in all things, even investment decisions. The days are evil, and time passes quickly, so attend to your resources responsibly before the Master returns.

Chapter 5

Set Free to Be Debt Free

Pay to all what is owed to them. . . .
Owe no one anything.
– Paul (Romans 13:7-8)

So far, we have explored essential principles for saving and investing. Now it is time to confront one of the greatest threats to financial health – debt. Credit allows us to conveniently purchase things using money we do not have. Getting into debt is quite easy, but it is extremely difficult to climb out of.

Debt is one of the most common and crippling burdens people carry. The pressure of owing more than we can repay is fuel for sleepless nights, strained marriages, missed opportunities, and overwhelming stress. Our culture tells us that debt is normal, even necessary, but God calls us to a better way.

Scripture consistently frames debt as a form of bondage. Solomon wrote: *The rich rules over the poor, and the borrower is the slave of the lender* (Proverbs 22:7). God wants His people to live in freedom, not in financial servitude. The only thing we should owe to others, according to Paul, is the debt of love, a debt because it is something we always owe to others (Romans 13:8).

While not all debt is avoidable, the path of wisdom is to move away from dependence on borrowed money and toward disciplined living. The decision you will make in this chapter is challenging, but it will usher in peace of mind while giving you the power to live generously and purposefully.

DECISION 5: I will avoid bad debt at all costs.

You cannot make real progress without a "zero tolerance" attitude toward bad debt and making purchases on credit, so let us look at some practical ways we can implement this decision.

1. Stop making bad debt a way of life.
You may be asking why we are suddenly adding "bad" in front of debt. Isn't all debt bad? The fact is, there is good debt and bad debt. You need to know the difference between the two and why you should do everything you can to avoid bad debt.

Good Debt – Good debt can work in your favor and be used to increase your future income. Business loans can lead to long-term wealth, student loans can help build a better, more lucrative career, and real estate can create equity and increase wealth. Good debt is debt that pays for itself, such as a rental property that covers the monthly mortgage payment through tenant rent while yielding a cash flow.

Bad Debt – Bad debt is consumer debt. It is bad because it steals from your future self to pay for your lifestyle today. Credit cards can be destructive to wealth building. Using credit often leads to impulse spending, and the high interest rates make those purchases more expensive than they seem. Car loans do the same because they encourage you to buy a vehicle that you really cannot afford. Payday loans or cash advance loans are the worst kinds of debt as they often carry interest rates as high as 300 percent (per annum).

When you allow debt to become a way of life, it becomes difficult – if not impossible – to build wealth. Debt costs you money; you pay a price in the form of interest. *You* are now working for your creditors; you have become the investment that makes others wealthy.

Unfortunately, the world around us bombards us with examples of bad financial decisions. Our government operates on such a severe deficit that the debt accrued over the past two decades has become almost insurmountable. Media and advertisements entice us with consumer products whose real costs are masked by seemingly "easy" payment options so that we can satisfy our need for immediate gratification. Easy access to social media increases covetousness and imitation because, in hopes of being more like those we follow and admire, we decide to spend, act, and dress like them. All of this sets the stage for poor financial choices that lead to bad debt.

Resolve today not to be a debtor. Stop using credit

cards, and do not even think about buying that SUV if you cannot afford to buy it with cash.

2. Always purchase consumer products with cash. Always!

As a life rule, do not purchase anything on credit that depreciates in value. If you are used to buying things on credit, it is time to make some fundamental behavioral changes.

Use cash for both small and big purchases. For example, if you are in the market to buy a car, there is no need to go into debt to do so. Save your money; buy a vehicle within your means and use cash. Yes, it does feel good to drive a new car. Buying new things tends to give us an emotional high, and a new car will certainly impress your friends. But if you take out a car loan to do so, you are making the bank investor rich, not you. And as soon as you drive a new car home, it depreciates in value by thousands of dollars. So, save up, buy a nice, pre-owned car, and you will save thousands of dollars in interest.

Pay for consumer products with cash whenever possible. Whole lending industries, like banks and credit card companies, profit by betting that you cannot resist buying consumer goods and paying them needless interest. But you *can* resist!

Credit card companies spend huge amounts of money trying to entice new customers. Brands like American Express spend millions in marketing expenses every year mailing solicitations to potential customers.

These credit card issuers do not care about *you* or *your* future. They are not doing *you* a favor. They care about *themselves* and *their* future. They want you to use their cards, carry a balance, pay exorbitant interest fees, and make them profitable. Resist their bait.

Credit card companies are businesses, and their goal is to make money. They are not concerned with your financial stability. Your debt is a liability for you but an asset for them. This does not necessarily make them evil, but you need wisdom and understanding of how they operate so that you can avoid the debt trap that could cripple you for years and severely detract from your potential wealth.

3. Discipline yourself to buy only things you need.

Buying things can be exciting, and part of the thrill of making credit card purchases is that they remove the immediate sting of parting with your money. Delaying payment removes the natural resistance of making the purchase.

A recent study indicates that buying on credit does more than ease a shopper's inhibitions – it actively encourages purchases. According to the study, when people shop with credit cards and see a product they like, the neural network in the brain that produces a sensation of reward perks up and seems to create a craving to spend.

The study showed that shoppers feel more rewarded when they shop with credit cards as opposed to cash. Even more concerning is that their brain becomes conditioned to spend. Over time, after repeated credit card purchases, the brain begins to associate credit card shopping with pleasure and anticipation.[6]

When you make purchases with cash, you feel the reduction in your bank account. The experience of buying with credit gives you a sense of pleasure, like you are getting something for nothing. It may feel good in the moment, but when all your spending catches up with you, leaving a large credit card balance, it hurts.

We do not like hearing the word *no*. Even in infancy, we recognize and understand it, and it is always unsettling and painful. And it is even harder to say no to ourselves. It is a struggle we face when trying to develop the virtues of discipline and self-control.

Godly stewards know how to say no to things they do not really need. They also know that certain luxuries like boats, jet skis, RVs, and off-road vehicles require storage space, insurance, and maintenance – costs beyond the price tag. Good stewards ask themselves: Does this really add value and freedom to my life, or is it just another burden?

As you pursue financial stability and wealth, discipline yourself to buy only the things that are essential for your well-being. A meal charged to a credit card might feel good in the moment, but if it leads to long-term debt, you will pay for it in the long run.

4. Make it hard for yourself to use credit cards.

It is vital to quash impulse spending. Online stores

---

6   Cheryl Winokur Munk, "How Credit Cards Affect Our Brains – and Our Spending," *Wall Street Journal*, May 1, 2021, https://www.wsj.com/finance/investing/how-credit-cards-affect-our-brainsand-our-spending-11619888401

make impulse buying easy, especially if your credit card information is saved to your internet browser. It is best to disable this feature; this forces you to retrieve your card and enter all the payment information manually. If you use Amazon's one-click feature, you may want to disable this feature as well. The one-click feature is convenient, but it makes it too easy to buy things. Going through the regular checkout process will make it more tedious to make a purchase.

This impulsivity is not original to us. We are all naturally born with a propensity to act on impulse. We inherited this from our first parents, Adam and Eve, who could not say no to a tempting fruit. They did not consider the eternal consequences of debt payment that would be imposed by disobeying God's command. The serpent convinced them to indulge now and pay later, but how great was the compounded cost of consuming that one product? Eve was deceived by her eyes, her body, her mind, her immediate desires, and her vulnerability to evil influences (Genesis 3:6).

Overall, Adam and Eve failed at appropriate values assessment and consequence evaluation. They bought on credit but did not have the means to pay when the debt came due, thus condemning all mankind. Had they trusted the word of God and exercised self-control, things would have gone differently.

Credit cards, poor money management, and impulse purchases all stem from the same root of covetousness. It is not wrong to desire things, but when those desires dominate our thoughts and drive our decisions, both the desire and actions resulting from the desire are wrong. Self-control combats covetousness and can help us resist using credit cards. It is a necessary virtue of godly stewardship and a defense against our adversary, the devil, who is still seeking those he can devour and distract from being useful for God (1 Peter 5:8). Money can be your tool for good or Satan's tool for evil.

As you commit to live beneath your means, take necessary measures to quell your shopping impulse.

5. Pay down credit card balances and eliminate all bad debt.

In your journey to build wealth, you will need to create a plan to reduce and eliminate all bad debt. You may be eager to invest your money in the stock market, but it is wise to pay off bad debt first. It makes little financial sense to earn 8 percent interest on an investment when you are paying 18 percent interest or more on a credit card balance.

A strong debt reduction plan includes several key steps:

Make a list of your debts from smallest to largest.

Most people do not realize how much debt they have. Collect all your credit card and loan statements, including the remaining balance you have on a car loan. List these debts from smallest to largest.

Pay off your smallest debts first.

While you will make minimum payments on all debts each month, your goal is to begin to pay off your smallest debt first. After you pay your smallest debt, move to the next smallest debt and work to pay it off in full as well. You will notice that as you pay off your smaller debts, you will have more money in the ensuing months to tackle the larger debts.

Close your credit card accounts.

Contact the banks or companies that issued your credit cards and cancel your accounts. If they offer you a better interest rate to coax you to keep your account, take them up on their offer. Ask for a better interest rate with no annual fee. This will save you money as you work toward paying off the balance. Once you have the new interest rate locked in, you can call back later and close the account, but do not make more purchases just because you have a lower interest rate!

Include your debt reduction plan in your budget.

If you are in debt, it is vital to allocate a portion of your income each month toward debt reduction and elimination. Be sure to write your debt reduction plan into your monthly budget. (See *Resource 1: Budget Worksheet.*)

When you are no longer in debt, you can then reallocate that monthly payment you were making to your savings and investment plan. In other words, you will make the shift from making payments to saving payments.

Consider selling a costly vehicle.

If you have a car loan with a large balance or if your monthly car payment is binding, you might consider selling your vehicle and getting rid of the payment altogether – even if you owe more than the car is worth. Paying off the loan and buying a modest, used vehicle with cash can free you from those heavy monthly payments.

This fifth decision, *I will avoid bad debt at all costs,* will set you free from unnecessary financial burdens. It, along with the other decisions, will empower you to devote more of your time, energy, and resources to what truly matters – blessing others and advancing God's kingdom.

Chapter 6

The Risk-Free Investment: Giving to the Lord

Honor the LORD with your wealth and with the firstfruits of all your produce; then your barns will be filled with plenty, and your vats will be bursting with wine.
– Solomon (Proverbs 3:9-10)

We have challenged you to make some big decisions on this journey. Most have been about earning, managing, and saving money. Now it is time to focus on the importance of *giving* back to the Lord.

Giving, as you will see, is even more important than saving, for it is an act of worship, an expression of trust, and a declaration that our hope is not in riches but in the One who richly provides.

God is the ultimate giver. He gave us His Son, His Spirit, and *every good and every perfect gift* we enjoy

(James 1:17). As stewards of His grace and provision, we are called to reflect His generosity with our finances. Supporting the work of the gospel, caring for the poor, and blessing others are all ways we store up treasure in heaven (Matthew 6:20). Generosity shifts our focus from self to service and from temporal wealth to eternal impact.

We pray you will make the following decision, not as an occasional act, but as a consistent, lifelong commitment:

DECISION 6: I will give generously to the work of the Lord.

One of the most profound decisions we can make is to give the first part of our earnings to the Lord. This act is called tithing, and it makes sense to give Him back a portion of our income since it came from Him in the first place. Tithing is an important biblical principle, and God blesses those who follow it.

Tithing Is Worship, Not Obligation

Tithing is not a "monthly payment" to God, a financial obligation similar to paying bills or fulfilling a financial duty. This perspective robs tithing of its true spiritual significance and reduces it to a transactional act. Tithing is an act of worship, a joyful expression of gratitude for God's provision. It is an offering of the first and best portion and expresses thanks to the Lord (Deuteronomy 26:10). When we tithe, we acknowledge that everything we have belongs to God (Psalm 24:1) and we are merely stewards of His resources. Think of tithing not in terms of how much of yours is given to the Lord but, rather, how much of His you are willing to keep for yourself. Tithing is not about meeting a requirement but about cultivating a heart of generosity and trust in God's faithfulness.

The Old Testament Tithe

This principle of tithing is rooted in the Old Testament. The first mention of tithing appears in Genesis when Abram gave Melchizedek, priest of God Most High, *a tenth of everything* (Genesis 14:20). Later, Jacob vowed to give *a full tenth* to the Lord of all that the Lord gave him (Genesis 28:22).

God required the Israelites to give 10 percent of their produce, livestock, and income back to Him (Leviticus 27:30-32). This tithe supported the Levites, who served in the temple, and provided for the poor, widows, and orphans (Deuteronomy 14:28-29). God commanded the Israelites: *"Bring the full tithe into the storehouse, that there may be food in my house"* (Malachi 3:10). The tithe was a tangible reminder of God's ownership over the land, its produce, and its people, and Israel's responsibility to Him as His tenants. It was a way for Israel to prove God's faithfulness and favor, that He would *open the windows of heaven* and pour out blessing until there was no more need (Malachi 3:10).

The 10 percent standard is a good principle to follow even today because it offers a clear baseline for giving.

However, the tithe in the Old Testament was not the ceiling of generosity but the floor – a starting point that demonstrated obedience and faith.

When God ordered the construction of the tabernacle, He asked from the people a contribution, or freewill offering, from everyone *whose heart moves him* (Exodus 25:2). When the people came with their offerings, they brought so much that Moses had to restrain the people because their gifts were *sufficient to do all the work, and more* (Exodus 36:7). God had provided the material originally when the Israelites, as slaves, plundered the Egyptians and left Egypt with an abundance of wealth and riches (Exodus 12:35-36). God always provides for the work He commands; we just need to be willing to obey.

New Testament Generosity

As New Testament believers, we are no longer under the Law but are called to give freely and generously, driven by love and gratitude rather than obligation. Paul wrote: *The point is this: whoever sows sparingly will also reap sparingly, and whoever sows bountifully will also reap bountifully. Each one must give as he has decided in his heart, not reluctantly or under compulsion, for God loves a cheerful giver* (2 Corinthians 9:6-7).

So, how much should we give?

Generosity in the New Testament is not bound by a specific percentage but is motivated by the grace we have received in Christ. This grace often inspires believers to tithe beyond 10 percent, reflecting the abundant giving modeled by Jesus, who gave His all for us (John 3:16).

Giving Generously beyond the Tithe

In addition to giving money to the local church for the work of the Lord, the Bible encourages us to give offerings to causes that align with God's heart for justice, mercy, and compassion. Proverbs 19:17 says, *Whoever is generous to the poor lends to the* LORD, *and he will repay him for his deed.* The thought of lending to the Lord should stir in us a genuine desire to be generous to those in need.

Paul commended the example of the Macedonians who, though not as wealthy as those in the Corinthian church, *overflowed in a wealth of generosity* and gave *beyond their means, of their own accord* (2 Corinthians 8:2-3) in a fervent desire to aid the work of the gospel. This heart attitude was fostered, Paul continued, because *they gave themselves first to the Lord and then by the will of God to us* (2 Corinthians 8:5). The heart is the key to godly giving.

The Macedonian believers had committed themselves wholly to the Lord, so when a need arose for the sake of the gospel, they were already primed to give. God accepts our giving as if we are offering it directly to Him. This giving can be directed toward missions, support for local ministries, and organizations that minister to the *least of these* (Matthew 25:40).

The early church recognized the call to serve the practical needs of the poor among them. Those who had believed the gospel *were of one heart and soul, and no one said that any of the things that belonged to him was his own. . . . There was not a needy person among them* as their offerings were *distributed to each as any had need* (Acts 4:32-35). Transformation by the power of the gospel creates in us a compassionate heart for others, and giving is a way to love our neighbor.

Tithing is a responsibility of every believer and the means by which God has prepared the funding of His work on earth. Paul told the Corinthians to put aside an offering on the first day of every week, *as he may prosper* (1 Corinthians 16:2). In other words, give according to how God has provided for you. As giving is tied to our worship on the first day of every week, we should be consistent and regular with our tithing. And we should determine the amount based on what God has given. Just as in the Old Testament, the tithe and offering helped support the Levites who had no land inheritance, the New Testament church has a responsibility to support the pastors, teachers, evangelists, and missionaries who have given up secular employment and committed their life and labor to the preaching of God's Word.

The Philippians partnered with Paul to supply his financial and practical needs *once and again* so that the fruit of that support could be realized in the salvation of souls (Philippians 4:16). Paul called their gift *a fragrant offering, a sacrifice acceptable and pleasing to God* (Philippians 4:18). John wrote that those who *have gone out for the sake of the name* ought to be supported by the church *that we may be fellow workers for the truth* (3 John 7-8). Your tithe in the Lord's hands can reap eternal dividends as an investment in the gospel.

I serve on the board of trustees of several Christian nonprofit organizations that meet needs as they advance the gospel. In one particular organization, Genesis College and Seminary, I work with a team of people who dedicate their time, talents, and financial resources to provide Bible training to inmates across the United States, free of charge. We currently have over 25000 inmates in 37 states enrolled in our courses. The members of the board and the advisory council give generously to this ministry without receiving any remuneration. Our reward is hearing testimony after testimony of men and women whose lives are being transformed by the power of the gospel. None of us regrets the time or the money we have invested in this ministry.

Allow God to direct your giving. As you pray about the amount to give, remember Paul's words: *Whoever sows bountifully will also reap bountifully* (2 Corinthians 9:6).

One Christian author is a notable example of extraordinary generosity. After receiving vast proceeds from a bestseller, he and his wife decided to implement a reverse tithe, giving 90 percent of their income and living on the remaining 10 percent. This decision was rooted in their belief that God had blessed them abundantly, and they wanted to use their resources to further His kingdom.

The author explained that the more he gave, the more his heart aligned with God's purposes and the less he depended on material wealth for contentment. His giving is a modern-day testimony to the truth of Christ's words: *It is more blessed to give than to receive* (Acts 20:35). While God may not be calling us to give 90 percent of our income, the author's generosity challenges us to view giving not as a duty but as an opportunity to partner with God in blessing others.

Jesus told a story about a poor widow who gave her last penny to the temple ministry. He did not criticize her for being wasteful or imprudent; instead, He praised her sacrifice: *And a poor widow came and put in two small copper coins, which make a penny. And he called his disciples to him and said to them, "Truly, I say to you, this poor widow has put in more than all those who are contributing to the offering box. For they contributed out of their abundance, but she out of her poverty has put in everything she had, all she had to live on"* (Mark 12:42-44).

Jesus is not saying that everyone should give everything away. The point is, if we only give out of our surplus, comfort, or convenience, it may feel good, but we are not *truly* giving because it did not really cost us anything. The value of something given is often assessed by what it cost the giver, and that cost borne by the giver reflects the value he places on the recipient. God wants us to give generously and sacrificially because He is that kind of giver. He gave "everything He had" for us. To reflect the truth that Christ, not our money or possessions, is our joy, we must be givers like Him – both to God and to others.

A Call to Generous Living

The sixth decision that leads to financial security and blessings, *I will give generously to the work of the Lord*, comes with no risk but a high reward. There is some level of risk with worldly investments, but when you sow into God's kingdom, you unlock heaven's resources. As Jesus said, *"Give, and it will be given to you. Good measure, pressed down, shaken together, running over, will be put into your lap"* (Luke 6:38). Jesus used this illustration from the marketplace, where grain was poured out, pressed down, and then filled to overflowing so that the buyer received every bit he paid for. In the same way, those who give generously will have a full and abundant measure paid back to them.

If you have never tithed before, start with small steps. Begin with 10 percent of your income. Give faithfully, give regularly, and watch how God provides. Pray over your tithe, asking God to use it for His glory and to deepen your trust in Him. If you already tithe, challenge yourself to give beyond the tithe. Seek opportunities to bless others, give to meaningful Christ-focused causes, and invest in God's kingdom generously.

As you trust God with your finances, you will discover that giving to the work of the Lord is an investment that is never a risk. The return on this investment is immeasurable – not only in financial provision but also in the joy and peace that come from walking in obedience to God's Word.

Chapter 7

The Power of Action

Whoever is slothful will not roast his game,
but the diligent man will get precious wealth.
– Solomon (Proverbs 12:27)

As we come to the end of our wealth-building journey together, we want to remind you that the decisions in this book are not meant merely for personal gain – a nicer house, a comfortable life, and a more secure retirement. They are about something far greater.

We were not created for comfort but for calling. Every breath we take and every resource we manage is an opportunity to serve others and advance God's kingdom. The real question is not what I want to do with my life and money, but what God wants to do through me.

Everything shifts when we understand that we are stewards and not owners. We begin to see our jobs, our homes, our bank accounts, and even our investment portfolios as tools for mission. We are here to reach the lost, bless others, build up the church, and bring glory to God. That is not a side project – it is the purpose of our lives. And when we live with that perspective, our efforts produce lasting fruit and eternal reward. Our lives and resources exist for God's kingdom and the good of others.

The last decision we are inviting you to make is about taking action:

> *DECISION 7: I will make a lasting covenant to invest my time, talents, and treasures to bless others and build God's kingdom.*

Faith with Action

Building wealth and stewarding resources wisely is not just about gaining knowledge and setting smart goals; it is also about living out your faith with action. The seventh decision is more than a statement of intention – you are deciding to live in alignment with God's will.

The Bible teaches us that faithfulness is the foundation for managing God's resources. Paul wrote: *It is required of stewards that they be found faithful* (1 Corinthians 4:2). That word *required* reminds us that faithfulness is not optional. We are commanded to be consistent and conviction-driven to honor God with our time, talents, and treasures.

Our *time* is a resource that cannot be replenished, and how we invest it reveals what we truly value. The *talents* we possess come from God, enabling us to serve others and glorify Him. And our *treasures* empower us to meet needs and advance God's work.

When we are faithful with these resources, we acknowledge that all we have belongs to God and must be used for His purposes. Consider Nehemiah, who showed unwavering faithfulness as he led the effort to rebuild Jerusalem's walls. He prayed, planned strategically, and worked tirelessly despite opposition. Like Nehemiah, we are called to build – not just material wealth – but legacies that reflect God's heart. Whether we are starting a business, investing wisely, or giving generously, it is our faithfulness and diligence that will ensure lasting fruit and bring honor to God.

Blessing Others through Our Actions

Scripture reminds us that just as Jesus laid down His life for us, so we must lay down our lives for others (1 John 3:16). What does this look like? John wrote, *If anyone has the world's goods and sees his brother in need, yet closes his heart against him, how does God's love abide in him?* (1 John 3:17). He then called believers to action: *Little children, let us not love in word or talk but in deed and in truth* (1 John 3:18).

When we invest in others, we reflect the love and sacrifice of Christ and create ripple effects of transformation. When you support a missionary, for example, you never know how that act of giving can compound in the future. Consider this: Our father[7] served as a missionary to India in the 1960s, planting churches throughout the

---

7   The authors of this book are siblings.

country. Those who supported him financially have most likely passed away, as has our father, but the investment they made in him still lives on today. These churches still exist, and thousands have come to Christ across several generations because faithful believers chose to give. Every act of giving is not only an investment but a fulfillment of the call to love God wholeheartedly and seek the highest good of our neighbor (Matthew 22:37, 39).

Making a Covenant of Stewardship

One of the most powerful ways we can live a life of godly stewardship is to write and keep a *Covenant of Stewardship*. This will translate good intentions to actionable steps, ensuring that stewardship becomes a lived reality, not just an idea. It is a declaration that you are committed to God and to faithfully stewarding the resources He has given you. A Covenant of Stewardship is not a legalistic bond but represents a heartfelt dedication to intentionally invest time, skills, and finances in ways that bless others and expand God's kingdom.

A Covenant of Stewardship has four basic parts: an acknowledgment of God's ownership, a statement of your role as steward, a description of your commitments, and your signature.

1. Begin by affirming that everything belongs to God. This establishes the foundation of your covenant. For example, "I acknowledge that everything I have belongs to the Lord, *for the earth is the LORD's and the fullness thereof*" (Psalm 24:1).

2. Clearly define your commitment as a caretaker of God's resources, recognizing your responsibility to manage them wisely (1 Corinthians 4:2). For example, "As His steward, I commit to managing all resources entrusted to me – time, talents, and finances – with diligence and integrity."

3. Outline the specific practices or principles you pledge to follow. This can include tithing, generosity, financial decisions, or supporting God's kingdom. For example, "I pledge to honor God by living generously, living within my means, building generational wealth, and investing in His kingdom. I will seek His wisdom in all decisions and glorify Him through faithful stewardship."

4. Signing your name and dating it makes your covenant official. If you are writing the covenant with your spouse, they should also sign it.

Here is an example of a stewardship covenant (next page):

As a family, we recognize that all we possess comes from God, the Creator of all things: The heavens are yours; the earth also is yours; the world and all that is in it, you have founded them (Psalm 89:11).

*We commit to being faithful stewards of His blessings by tithing to our church, practicing generosity, and using our time and talents to serve others. Proverbs 3:9-10 says, Honor the L*ORD *with your wealth and with the firstfruits of all your produce; then your barns will be filled with plenty, and your vats will be bursting with wine. Guided by this principle, we will honor the Lord with our wealth and resources and trust Him to direct our steps as we build a legacy of faithfulness for His glory.*

Signed: _____Date: _____

Once you draft the content, format it on your computer to look like a formal document. Use a large font size for the title, *Covenant of Stewardship*. Once you print it, sign it, and date it, you may want to frame it and display it somewhere where you will see it often.

Keep your covenant concise; it should fit on one page. Use clear, direct language, making the covenant memorable and meaningful. Also, be sure to incorporate Scripture, supporting your commitments with biblical principles and verses.

Make it personal. Write in first person to express your commitment sincerely and personally. Finally, pray as you write your covenant, and once you complete it, ask for God's guidance and strength to fulfill the commitments.

Making and living by this covenant will inspire consistency in giving, serving, and managing your resources wisely, even when circumstances make it challenging. It will help keep your focus on what really matters – investing in things with eternal value, such as spreading the gospel and meeting the needs of others. By faithfully keeping this covenant, you will glorify God as the true owner of all you have and align your life with the principles of God's Word.

Epilogue

You have been invited to make seven big decisions. If embraced, these decisions have the power to radically change your life and your future.

1. *I will make money a tool, not a treasure.*

2. *I will save money at all costs.*

3. *I will not let pleasure control me or distract me from faithfully stewarding God's resources.*

4. *I will invest the resources God has entrusted to me and let every dollar multiply.*

5. *I will avoid bad debt at all costs.*

6. *I will give generously to the work of the Lord.*

7. *I will make a lasting covenant to invest my time, talents, and treasures to bless others and build God's kingdom.*

If you choose to make these decisions, we believe according to Scripture that God will bless you, and you will be a blessing to others.

Planning for your financial future is wise and responsible but takes time and patience. Building wealth does not happen overnight. It requires living below your means, consistently investing, and staying committed to your plan for a long time – even if you feel like you are not making much progress.

Preparing for Your Eternal Future

As emphasized in this book, preparing for the years ahead involves strategy, sacrifice, planning, resource management, and patience. As vital as financial planning is, it pales in comparison to the importance of preparing for your eternal future. Earthly wealth and the state of your portfolio are temporary, but your relationship with God and the state of your soul carry eternal significance.

Scripture reminds us that life is fleeting: *What is your life? For you are a mist that appears for a little time and then vanishes* (James 4:14). Wealth and possessions make life comfortable on earth, but they do not secure what truly matters. Our earthly investments will eventually fade. Only what is done for God's glory will endure.

Preparing for your eternal future begins with acknowledging your need for salvation. God's Word teaches that every person has sinned and fallen short of God's standard (Romans 3:23). But through Jesus Christ, God offers us the gift of eternal life (Romans 6:23).

Planning for eternity involves more than just acknowledging God's existence; it requires a personal relationship with Him through faith in Jesus Christ.

Jesus said, *I am the way, and the truth, and the life. No one comes to the Father except through me* (John 14:6).

If you want to be certain that your eternal future is secure, do not close this book without surrendering your life to Christ. Place your faith in Jesus for the forgiveness of your sins and the promise of eternal life. The way to salvation begins with a simple decision: Will I receive Christ into my life, or will I reject Him? The Bible says that all who receive Jesus and believe in His name have *the right to become children of God* (John 1:12).

If you have never placed your faith in Christ, you can do so now. There are no prescribed words you must pray. Simply tell God you need Him and want to begin a relationship with Him. If you do not know what to say to God, here is a simple prayer to pray. This prayer will not save you; it simply provides some words that, if prayed in faith, will help you articulate your faith in Christ:

"God, I believe You love me. I know I am a sinner, but You gave Your only Son for me so that I can live forever with You and enjoy Your love for all eternity. By faith, I graciously receive Your gift of salvation. I am ready to trust You as my Lord and Savior. Amen."

If you made a decision to follow Christ, remember this day. Today is your spiritual birthday and the most important day of your life! By trusting in Jesus, you have secured a future that no economic downturn or earthly loss can take away.

As we close this book, we pray you will make the decisions in this book that lead to financial security and blessings. But as you work toward your financial goals, build your life on the foundation of Christ and align your priorities with God's will. Invest in God's kingdom, using your time, talents, and resources to advance His work on this earth. These investments have eternal value.

Finally, as you prioritize your eternal future, remember you are investing in something far greater than stocks or bonds – you are securing an inheritance that will never perish, spoil, or fade (1 Peter 1:4).

An Introductory Course on the Stock Market

What is the Stock Market?

The stock market is a collection of exchanges and markets where buyers and sellers trade stocks, bonds, and other securities. It serves as a platform for companies to raise capital by selling shares of ownership (equity) to investors and for investors to buy and sell these shares to achieve financial goals.

The stock market is vital to the economy because it provides businesses with the funding needed to grow and innovate while offering individuals and institutions opportunities to build wealth over time. Major stock exchanges in the United States include the New York Stock Exchange (NYSE) and the Nasdaq.

How Does the Stock Market Work?

The stock market operates through a network of exchanges where stocks are listed, traded, and regulated. Here is how it functions:

Stock Listings: Companies go public by offering shares of stock through an Initial Public Offering (IPO). These shares are then listed on exchanges for trading.

Trading: Investors buy and sell stocks through brokerage accounts. Trades occur when a buyer and seller agree on a price.

Prices: Stock prices fluctuate based on supply and demand but are influenced by company performance, economic indicators, and market sentiment.

Regulation: The Securities and Exchange Commission (SEC) ensures fair trading practices and market transparency.
The stock market is divided into two segments:

Primary Market: Where new securities are sold to investors.

Secondary Market: Where existing securities are traded among investors.

Major US Stock Market Indexes

Indexes are tools that measure the performance of specific segments of the stock market. They are crucial for tracking market trends, comparing individual investments, and assessing the economy's overall health. Here are some key US stock market indexes:

S&P 500 (Standard & Poor's 500)

Description: The S&P 500 tracks the performance of 500 of the largest publicly traded companies in the US across various industries.

Importance: It is widely regarded as a benchmark for the US stock market's overall health. It represents about 80 percent of the market's total value.

Dow Jones Industrial Average (DJIA)

Description: The DJIA tracks the performance of 30 large, well-established US companies known for their industry leadership.

Importance: While limited in scope, the DJIA is a popular indicator of economic trends and investor sentiment.

NYSE Composite Index

Description: This tracks all common stocks listed on the New York Stock Exchange.

Importance: It reflects the performance of a broad range of industries within the NYSE.

Nasdaq Composite Index

Description: This includes all stocks listed on the Nasdaq exchange, with a strong emphasis on technology and growth-oriented companies.

Importance: It is a leading indicator of innovation-driven industries, such as technology and biotechnology.

Russell 1000, 2000, and 3000 Indexes

Description:

Russell 1000 measures the performance of the 1,000 largest companies in the US.

Russell 2000 focuses on 2,000 smaller companies, providing insight into small-cap market performance.

Russell 3000 combines the Russell 1000 and 2000 to represent the total US stock market.

Importance: They offer a comprehensive view of large and small-cap companies and the market as a whole.

AMEX Market Value Index

Description: This tracks the performance of stocks listed on the American Stock Exchange (AMEX), focusing on small and mid-cap companies.

Importance: It highlights smaller, often more volatile companies less represented in larger indexes.

Why Understanding Stock Market Indexes Matters

For new investors, understanding stock market indexes is crucial for several reasons:

Benchmarking Performance: Indexes allow investors to compare their portfolio's performance against the broader market or specific sectors.

Risk Assessment: Different indexes represent varying levels of risk. For example, the Nasdaq's tech-heavy composition is more volatile than the S&P 500.

Diversification: Index funds and ETFs (Exchange-Traded Funds) often mirror the performance of these indexes, offering a cost-effective way to diversify investments.

Economic Indicators: Index movements reflect market trends and can signal shifts in economic conditions, helping investors make informed decisions.

Key Takeaways

The stock market is a dynamic and essential component of the global economy, offering individuals opportunities to grow wealth. By understanding the roles and characteristics of major stock indexes, new investors can:

- Gauge market trends
- Make informed investment choices
- Build diversified, resilient portfolios

For those just starting out, learning the basics of these indexes provides a solid foundation for navigating the complex yet rewarding world of investing.

Resource 1: Budget Worksheet

A budget helps you track your spending. Set specific spending limits for each category and commit to staying within them. Aim to reduce your expenses and to direct as much money as possible toward debt elimination and, ultimately, to savings and investment.

Budget for Month of _____		
Expenditures	Amount Budgeted	Amount Spent
Debt reduction/Elimination		
Savings/Investments		
Debt Payments (e.g., credit cards, auto loans, student loans)		
Unexpected Expenses		
Housing (e.g., rent/mortgage, property taxes)		
Insurance (e.g., homeowners, renters, auto, health)		
Transportation (e.g., gas, oil, Uber/Lyft)		
Utilities (e.g., electric, gas, sewer/trash, internet, cell)		
Groceries		
Dining Out (e.g., meals, coffee, refreshments)		
Entertainment (e.g., movie and music downloads, gaming)		
Clothing (e.g., clothes, shoes, dry cleaning)		
Personal Care (e.g., haircuts, nails, gym membership)		
Health Care (e.g., doctor visits, prescriptions)		
Gifts		
Education (e.g., tuition, books, supplies)		
Children (e.g., daycare, preschool, child support)		
Donations (e.g., tithes and offerings)		
Other		
Other		

Resource 2: Financial Goals Workshop

King Solomon wrote: *The plans of the diligent lead surely to abundance, but everyone who is hasty comes only to poverty* (Proverbs 21:5). The most successful people have plans, and they are careful to follow through with their plans. In this workshop, you will create short-term, mid-term, and long-term goals with corresponding action plans.

Here are the steps to create meaningful and effective financial goals:

Step 1: Pray for Guidance

Begin by seeking God's wisdom (Proverbs 3:5-6) to ensure your goals align with God's will.

Step 2: Prioritize

Identify which goals are most important to your financial and spiritual growth. For example, if you have not given faithfully to the work of the Lord, a possible goal might be: Commit to giving 10 percent of my income as a tithe to my local church.

Step 3: Determine Your Goals

It is helpful to think about the future and what you hope to accomplish in the long range. Once you determine this, you can break these long-term goals into mid-term and short-term goals to help you work toward your long-term objectives.

Here are some examples of short-term, mid-term, and long-term goals to help inspire your own possible goals:

Short-Term Goals (1 Year or Less)

Example 1: Create a budget in the next seven days and put it into use immediately.

Example 2: Save $1,000 over the next 12 months in an emergency fund to prepare for unexpected expenses and honor God's call to wisdom and foresight (Proverbs 21:20).

Mid-Term Goals (1 to 5 Years)

Example 1: Pay off $10,000 in consumer debt in the next three years, demonstrating responsible stewardship and avoiding enslavement to lenders (Proverbs 22:7).

Example 2: Save $12,000 per year over the next 5 years for a down payment on a home.

Long-Term Goals (5 Years or More)

Example 1: Work with a wealth manager to build a retirement fund sufficient to provide financial security while I continue to give generously in retirement.

Example 2: Establish a family foundation focused on kingdom-building initiatives.

Step 4: Create Action Steps for Each Goal

Break down each goal into 3 or 4 actionable tasks or steps. For each step, describe what needs to be done and how it will be carried out. It is wise to set deadlines for each task. Here is a sample goal with an action plan:

Goal: I will hold a garage sale with the goal of raising $400 toward my emergency fund.

Action Steps:

1. Set the date of the garage sale, making sure the date does not conflict with other plans.

2. Set aside 6 hours this Saturday to go through all the items that I no longer need or want.

3. List bigger items, like my acoustic guitar, on an online classified ad platform to get a jump start on the garage sale.

4. Make cardboard signs to display in my neighborhood to advertise the sale.

Step 5: Write Down Your Goals

Use the following template to assist you in creating short-term, mid-term, and long-term goals. You can write your goals in this book or simply write them on a separate piece of paper. Keep your goals visible to remind yourself of the important decisions you have made regarding your financial goals.

Short-term Goals

Goal 1: _____

Action Steps:

1. _____

2. _____

3. _____

4. _____

Goal 2: _____

Action Steps:

1. _____

2. _____

3. _____

4. _____

Mid-term Goals

Goal 1: _____

Action Steps:

1. _____

2. _____

3. _____

4. _____

Goal 2: _____

Action Steps:

    1. _____

    2. _____

    3. _____

    4. _____

Long-term Goals

Goal 1: _____

Action Steps:

    1. _____

    2. _____

    3. _____

    4. _____

Goal 2: _____

Action Steps:

    1. _____

    2. _____

    3. _____

    4. _____

Congratulations on completing this workshop! Establishing and maintaining financial goals are powerful ways to practice diligence, wisdom, and faithfulness in wealth building and stewardship.

Study Guide for *Investing Wisely*

Investing Wisely is a biblical guide for new investors who want to save diligently, invest strategically, and give generously. Each chapter equips readers to steward God's resources faithfully and build a life that honors Him and blesses others.

This study guide has been designed to help you execute the seven decisions that lead to financial security and blessings. Carefully answer all questions and complete all the exercises. As you invest the time to put these godly principles into action, you will position yourself to be blessed by God and to be a blessing to others.

Study Guide
Chapter 1: Money Is a Tool, Not a Treasure

In this first chapter, we challenged you to make the first life-changing decision:

I will make money a tool, not a treasure.

A wise steward understands that money is a resource to be used for God's purposes rather than an end in itself. Scripture teaches that earthly wealth is temporary and cannot compare to eternal treasures in heaven (Matthew 6:19-21). By thinking of money as a tool, we free ourselves from its grip, recognizing its greatest value lies in how it can serve others and glorify God. The decision to view money as a tool, not a treasure, redefines financial success. Such success is not about accumulation but strategically and faithfully managing our resources to advance God's kingdom.

The following will help you put this decision into practice:

Questions:

1. Money is a tool, not a treasure. What does this mean?

2. Jesus said, *"For where your treasure is, there your heart will be also"* (Matthew 6:21). What does it reveal about our values when money and possessions are our treasure? If you were to take an honest look at your life, what would you say is your greatest treasure?

3. In the story of the Rich Young Ruler, what indicates that money was his treasure, not a tool?

4. When Christ is your treasure, you live generously, trust completely, and live with eternity in mind. Of these three, which one is the most challenging for you? Why? How will you overcome this challenge?

Exercise: Keep Christ Your Treasure

Every Christian should be able to wholeheartedly say, "Christ is my treasure." But money and the things money can buy often distract us from making Christ the truest treasure of our lives. In addition to money and possessions, certain people, activities, and priorities can also take first place in our lives.

1. On a piece of paper, make a list of the things that have the potential to be a treasure in your life.

2. Next to each item, write down what you must do to ensure that these things do not become more precious to you than Christ.

3. Write a prayer that you can lift every day. The prayer might be for help to change your perspective of money, or it may be an affirmation that Christ is more valuable to you than anything else. Display your prayer in a place where you will see it and pray it every day.

Study Guide
Chapter 2: Every Dollar Counts

In this chapter, we invited you to make the second decision:

I will save money at all costs.

Saving is a foundational principle of wise financial stewardship. Proverbs 21:20 reminds us: *Precious treasure and oil are in a wise man's dwelling, but a foolish man devours it.* Committing to saving at all costs requires discipline and foresight, ensuring resources are available for future needs and unexpected challenges. This decision is a proactive step toward financial stability and freedom, enabling us to avoid debt, embrace generosity, and steward God's provisions with intentionality.

The following will help you put this decision into practice:

Questions:

1. There are three basic types of people: debtors, spenders, and savers. Which category would you put most of your friends into? Your parents? Which one of these categories best describes you?

2. Does the thought of living on a budget discourage or encourage you? Why? To be able to save money at all costs, are you willing to create a budget and faithfully live by it? Explain.

3. To help you reduce expenses so that you can

put money in a savings account, what are some tasks you can do yourself that you normally outsource? (e.g., washing your car, coloring your hair, making meals)

Exercise: Create a Budget

Using a budget is the best way to keep track of your money. This exercise will walk you through the process of creating one.

1. Follow these five preparatory steps to create a budget:

Step 1: Gather all your bills.

Step 2: Analyze your receipts or your checking/debit account statements. On a sheet of paper, create categories that specify how you spent your money last month (e.g., entertainment, eating out, transportation). Write down how much money you spent in each category. (Many banking apps will do this for you.)

Step 3: Review your pay stubs and the invoices from all streams of income you may have. Calculate your monthly income and write it down.

Step 4: Subtract your monthly expenses from your monthly income.

Step 5: Distinguish between needs and wants by writing an N next to needs and a W next to wants.

2. Go to Resource 1: Budget Worksheet and fill out this worksheet using the preparatory work you completed in the five steps above.

Estimate your income and expenses for the following month. Allocate money to the appropriate categories, keeping your needs in mind. Your goal is to budget your money so that you (a) increase money to pay off debts or add to your savings and investments and (b) decrease money spent on wants.

Keep working and reworking your budget so you can assign money to debt payments or savings and investments. Be sure to be realistic. It is no good to have a dream budget if you are unable to follow it.

3. If you do not have excess money to put toward debt or investments, consider starting a side hustle or finding a part-time job.

The importance of following a budget cannot be overstressed. Be disciplined. Make sacrifices, and be consistent.

Study Guide
Chapter 3: It Hurts, but the Pain Is Not in Vain

In this chapter, we encouraged you to make a third major decision:

> I *will not let pleasure control me or distract me from faithfully stewarding God's resources.*

Pleasure and comfort are tempting distractions that can erode financial discipline and stewardship. Ecclesiastes 5:10 warns: *He who loves money will not be satisfied with money, nor he who loves wealth with his income.* This decision acknowledges the danger of being controlled by desires and commits to placing eternal priorities over tempting indulgences. True contentment comes from living within God's plan for our resources, resisting the impulse to overspend, and staying focused on kingdom-minded goals.

The following will help you put this decision into practice:

Questions:

1. King Solomon said that whoever loves wine and olive oil will never become rich. What is your wine or olive oil? Make a list of the pleasurable items you habitually spend money on (e.g., expensive coffee drinks, bottled water, streaming services).

2. If you were to make a sacrifice and give up some

of the pleasurable items listed in your answer to Question 1, what obstacles would you need to overcome? (An obstacle might be a mindset: "I need this to function," or it might be an obligation, a lifestyle behavior, etc.) How will you overcome each obstacle so that pleasure does not control you or keep you from building wealth?

3. Who can hold you accountable to make sacrifices so that you can build wealth?

Exercise: Establish Financial Goals

Goal setting is a powerful way to convert your desires into action. Go to *Resource 2: Financial Goals Workshop* to create goals relating to debt elimination, savings/investments, and establishing potential streams of income.

1. Start with short-term goals. Create two goals that you can begin pursuing today. For each goal, create an action plan that describes how you will fulfill the goal.

2. Create mid-term and long-term goals. Now is the time to think about the future. You need to decide where you want to be financially and how you will get there. Be sure to create an action plan for each goal.

Review these goals regularly and make adjustments as needed.

Study Guide
Chapter 4: Every Dollar Compounds

In this chapter, we invited you to make a fourth decision:

I will invest the resources God has entrusted to me and let every dollar multiply.

Wise stewardship requires more than saving – it calls for intentional investment that multiplies resources. In Matthew 25:14-30, Jesus commends the servant who invests and increases his master's talents, illustrating the principle of fruitful stewardship. This decision reflects a commitment to letting every dollar work toward financial growth, providing future security, and increasing your capacity to be generous. Proper investment turns passive savings into active tools for advancing God's purposes and building long-term wealth.

The following will help you put this decision into practice:

Questions:

1. Warren Buffett lived by a principle called the Methuselah Technique. Why is it important to think about your investments in terms of this principle?

2. Why is the stock market a good option for new investors with limited assets? Note: If you decide to invest in the stock market using an online trading platform, educate yourself on the company's terms and conditions. And always remember that

these investments involve risk. It is possible to lose money in the stock market.

3. What are the benefits of diversification?

4. What guidelines for investing will you create to ensure your investment approach aligns with your biblical beliefs and convictions?

Exercise 1: How Compound Interest Works

Compound interest is earning interest on your interest. To determine the future value of an investment, use the compound interest formula: $P(1 + r)^t$

P = principal

r = interest rate

t = time

Follow the steps below to learn how to use this formula. These steps will walk you through a $3,000 investment (P) at a 15 percent interest rate (r) after 10 years (t): $3,000(1 + .15)^{10}$.

Step 1: Add 1 to the interest rate (decimal form). For example, add 1 to .15 which equals 1.15.

Step 2: Using the number of years as an exponent, raise the total from step 1 (1.15) to the t power (10): $(1.15)^{10} = 4.05$. (This number was rounded to two decimal places.)

Step 3: Multiply this total by the principal invested ($3,000): 4.05 X 3,000 = $12,150.

So, if you invest $3,000 at an interest rate of 15 percent

and let it sit for 10 years, your total investment will be valued at $12,500. Your $3,000 earned an additional $9,150 without any effort from you.

Now it is your turn.

1. How much would a $1,000 investment be worth after 10 years at a 13 percent interest rate?

2. How much would a $5,000 investment be worth after 15 years at a 12 percent interest rate?

3. How much would a $600 investment be worth after 20 years at a 24 percent interest rate?

ANSWER KEY (Your totals may vary slightly due to rounding.)

1. $3,390
2. $27,350
3. $44,316

Exercise 2: Investigate Online Trading Platforms

1. Use the internet to search for online trading platforms that have low or no minimum requirements to open an account. Make a list of these companies.

2. After reading the terms and conditions of each of these companies, decide if any of these online trading platforms are right for you.

Please note: If you choose to open an account, be aware of the inherent risk involved. It is possible to hit a downturn and lose your entire investment. (Diversification typically minimizes the risk.)

Study Guide
Chapter 5: Set Free to Be Debt Free

In this chapter, we invited you to make the following decision:

I will avoid bad debt at all costs.

Living within one's means is a cornerstone of financial wisdom. Proverbs 22:7 cautions: *The borrower is the slave of the lender*, reminding us of the burdens of debt. This decision to spend only what is available – and only what is necessary – builds contentment and guards against financial ruin. It cultivates a lifetime of moderation and prudence, empowering us to prioritize stewardship over materialism and freeing us to pursue generosity with a clear conscience.

The following will help you put this decision into practice:

Questions:

1. What are the differences between good and bad debt?

2. How will you discipline yourself to use only cash and not credit cards?

3. What can you do to make it hard for yourself to use credit cards?

Exercise: Debt Elimination

It is advisable to pay off all your bad debts before beginning to invest. Here are some action steps to help you reduce and eliminate bad debts:

1. Make a list of all your bad debts along with the balance of each debt. (You may also want to write down the interest rate that you are paying on each debt to remind you that *you* are the investment that is making *others* wealthy.)

2. Arrange the debts from smallest to largest.

3. Decide how aggressively you will pay off the smallest debt. Be sure that your decision is reflected in your budget.

4. If your smallest debt is to a credit card company, obtain their contact information so you can cancel this card. If they offer you a lower interest rate to keep your business, take them up on their offer, but resolve to no longer use this card.

Repeat steps 3 and 4 until all your debts have been paid off.

Study Guide
Chapter 6: The Risk-Free Investment:
Giving to the Lord

In this chapter, we challenged you to make a sixth life-changing decision:

> *I will give generously to the work of the Lord.*

Generosity reflects the heart of God, who gave His only Son to us (John 3:16). This decision recognizes that giving is not a loss but a spiritual investment with eternal returns. Faithful giving to God's work advances His kingdom, meets the needs of others, and deepens our trust in His provision. Generosity turns wealth into worship, making it a powerful act of obedience and love.

The following will help you put this decision into practice:

Questions:

1. What is tithing, and why is it important? Do you faithfully give to the work of the Lord? Why or why not?

2. How does acknowledging that all things belong to God change the way you view giving?

3. Paul wrote: *The point is this: whoever sows sparingly will also reap sparingly, and whoever sows bountifully*

will also reap bountifully (2 Corinthians 9:6). What did Paul mean in this verse?

4. Paul continued: *Each one must give as he has decided in his heart, not reluctantly or under compulsion, for God loves a cheerful giver* (2 Corinthians 9:7). What is the Lord saying to you about giving?

Exercise: Set a Giving Goal

This chapter emphasized the biblical call to invest generously in God's kingdom. In the Study Guide Exercise for Chapter 3, you established several financial goals. Now we are inviting you to set a giving goal related to the work of the Lord. This goal may be about faithfully tithing, giving beyond the tithe, giving generously to those in need, or whatever God places on your heart. The amount is between you and the Lord. For help in establishing this goal, use the worksheet in *Resource 2: Financial Goals Workshop.*

Chapter 7: The Power of Action

In this chapter, we challenged you to make the seventh and final decision:

I will make a lasting covenant to invest my time, talents, and treasures to bless others and build God's kingdom.

A life of purpose flows from a commitment to use all that we have for God's glory. Romans 12:1 urges us to offer ourselves as living sacrifices, holy and pleasing to God. The decision to make a covenant is not a legalistic bond but a heartfelt resolution to invest your time, skills, and finances in ways that bless God and others. It helps us shift our focus from personal gain to eternal impact, aligning every resource with the divine mission of love, stewardship, and service.

The following will help you put this decision into practice:

Questions:

1. Chapter 7 begins with a quote from Proverbs 12:27: *Whoever is slothful will not roast his game, but the diligent man will get precious wealth.* What important principle did Solomon emphasize in this verse?

2. How is investing in others a reflection of the love and sacrifice of Christ?

3. Are you apprehensive, excited, or indifferent about making a Covenant of Stewardship? Explain.

Exercise: Write Your Covenant

You learned how to create a Covenant of Stewardship in Chapter 7. Now it is time to draft your own document. As you write the covenant, remember to include all four parts:

1. An acknowledgement of God's ownership (Psalm 24:1)

2. A statement of your role as a steward

3. A description of your commitments

4. Your signature

Refer to the chapter for examples of appropriate wording but be sure to make your covenant true to your convictions and commitments. Once you have completed your covenant, print it, sign and date it, and display it somewhere where you will see it often.

About the Authors

David N. Johnson

David was born and raised in California and married his childhood sweetheart, Lisa, in 1986. They have three wonderful daughters and nine amazing grandchildren. He has been a wealth manager since 1990 with the Series 7, 63, 65, and 24 licenses, and founded Johnson Wealth Management in 1994. When they are at their Arizona or Texas homes, they are active in their local church, Rotary, and several boards and foundations. They also love to travel to visit their children and grandchildren around the country.

www.jwealth.co

J. A. Johnson

Dr. J. A. Johnson is a founding member of Genesis College & Seminary, an international ministry serving thousands of inmates across the nation. He has also served as a faculty member at Christian colleges and universities. Dr. Johnson is blessed with four wonderful children and six cherished grandchildren.

www.genesisbibleinstitute.org